*The early years of*
*Brian O'Nolan / Flann O'Brien / Myles na gCopaleen*

*The early years of*

# BRIAN O'NOLAN
/
# FLANN O'BRIEN
/
# MYLES na gCOPALEEN

Ciarán Ó Nualláin
/
*Translated from the Irish by Róisín Ní Nualláin*
/
*Edited by Niall O'Nolan*

THE LILLIPUT PRESS
DUBLIN

First published 1998 by
THE LILLIPUT PRESS LTD
62-63 Sitric Road, Arbour Hill,
Dublin 7, Ireland.
e-mail: lilliput@indigo.ie
http://indigo.ie/~lilliput

A CIP record for this
title is available from
The British Library.

ISBN 1 901866 18 1

The Lilliput Press receives financial assistance from
An Chomhairle Ealaíon/The Arts Council of Ireland.

The bottom photo on the front cover is from a portrait of Brian O'Nolan
by Micheál O'Nolan and is reproduced courtesy of Boston College.
Other images reproduced courtesy of the O'Nolan family.

Set in 12 on 15 Lapidary by Sheila Stephenson
Printed in England by MPG Books Ltd of Cornwall

# Contents

# Illustrations

*Brian O'Nolan's mother, née Agnes Gormley, holding her first-born, Gearóid.*

# 1

MY FATHER AND MOTHER both came from Omagh in
County Tyrone, but it was in another Tyrone town, Strabane,
that they were to meet and marry. My father, Michael, was
born in 1875 at Mullach Mór, a couple of miles outside
Omagh. His mother, one of the Melon family, came from
Eiscir Dufaigh, a townland near Newtown. While Michael was
young the family moved to Belfast, where he got most of his
education in St Malachy's College. In 1897, having taken a
university degree, he joined the civil service in Customs and
Excise. Travel and frequent relocation were a part of that job
and at the turn of the new century he was based in Strabane.
It was during his posting in Strabane that he began to teach
Irish, holding evening classes in the town and in neighbouring
districts. He had perfected his own Irish in Cloch Cheannaola
and on Tory Island in County Donegal. The level of enthusi-
asm and interest in his classes is indicated by a file of books
ordered from the Gaelic League in the years 1902 and 1903 –
75 copies of O'Growney's *Lessons* and 25 copies of *Greann na*

*Gaeilge*. In 1903 he organized a Feis in Strabane – the first such event ever held in that part of the country. One of his notebooks dating from that time contains an outline of a play, in English.

My mother, Agnes Gormley, was born in Castle Street, Omagh, in 1886. Her father, John Gormley, had a shop in Omagh, but moved his family to Strabane the following year and opened a stationer's shop in Market Street.

The Gormley business prospered and within a short time John Gormley acquired a site on Main Street on which he erected a fine building that combined a substantial shop and dwelling-house. Both shops remained in the Gormley family until the 1960s.

It is surprising how quickly people meet one another, particularly in a small town. I do not know whether it was in the shop or at one of the Irish classes that my father and mother first met, but in any event they were married in 1906 in the parish church of Murloch, near Strabane. Michael's two

*Michael Victor O'Nolan*

brothers, Father Gearóid and Father Peter, assisted two of the local priests in the ceremony, which was conducted for the most part in Irish – 'an interesting departure', as the *Derry Journal* commented in its report of the wedding. A decorative delph plate carrying the inscription 'A gift from Clann na nGaodhal, a branch of the Gaelic League, Robstown, to M.V. Ó Nualláin on the occasion of his marriage, September 1906' always held a prominent place in the family china cabinet.

Father Gearóid, who was Professor of Irish at St Patrick's College, Maynooth, recorded some background to the earlier days of our father and his three sisters, whom we never met because they all died while still very young. In an autobiographical book, *Beatha Duine a Thoil*, long since out of print, Father Gearóid records some family history.

Our paternal grandfather, Dónall Ó Nualláin, was Professor of Music at Omagh's Model School, and the girl that he was to marry was a pupil at that school. She was only eighteen years of age when they married. Her family, as far as we know, still farm near Newtown. Our father had seven siblings: Gearóid, Fergus, Peadar, Pádraig, Máire, Eibhlís and Caitlín.

After their marriage our grandparents went to live in a country house at Dearg Muine, a couple of miles from Omagh. Later they moved to Mullach Mór, a mile outside the town, and it was here that our father was born. A few years later the family moved back into Omagh and Michael and Gearóid were sent to school in Cill an Chlochair. Hardly settled in Omagh, the family had to be uprooted once again on their father's transfer to Belfast.

'I do not remember much about Michael's school days but I do recall some things about our life at home,' wrote Father

Gearóid. 'Michael was a wonderful storyteller. Often when we were in bed we would prevail on him to tell a story and he would respond readily. He had a great imagination and tales of the *Arabian Nights* and others of his own invention were equally exciting to us.'

Probably it is a coincidence that we had similar habits when we were children, for it would fall to me to do the storytelling every night. I had learned to read on my own initiative by the age of six and it is likely that my reading material became the source of my stories.

Michael's mother hoped that he would become a clerical student as his brother Gearóid was. She was disappointed when he told her that he had no such vocation and that he intended to marry. 'He did well at whatever examinations he took,' according to Father Gearóid, 'and was awarded a special prize for English composition.' Michael began work as a civil servant in Belfast but served in many other towns. Gearóid recalls an incident when Michael took a train one Sunday from Belfast to a small town twenty-three miles from

*Father Gearóid, Brian's uncle*

the city. For some reason he missed the train back, and as he had to open a certain distillery at nine o'clock next morning he had to walk the twenty-three miles home! The following day he was cycling in the city and was involved in a collision with a carriage, which knocked him down. He got up and continued his journey but reported the following day that he felt as though a steamroller had crushed him. Whether it was the long walk or the fall from the bicycle, our father suffered no long-term ill effects. He was a great walker like his brother Pádraig; neither of them would have considered twenty miles a challenge.

Half the family died young – Pádraig and the three girls. Pádraig was hardly twenty when he died of tuberculosis. He had a keen interest in Irish and won first prize for recitation at a local Feis when he was fifteen. Máire and Eibhlís also succumbed to tuberculosis. In his account Father Gearóid found it hard to explain their early deaths as there had been no history of TB in either family or in their forebears. Today it is not difficult to understand the tragedy that affected so many families. We know now that the root of TB was not in the blood or bone but in the milk. In many a country district the population suffered because of a single diseased cow.

Caitlín, the youngest girl, died of diabetes. She was a teacher and a fine girl, judged by her photograph. In those days there was no cure for diabetes. When it was evident that she was seriously ill and unlikely to recover, Father Gearóid brought her to Uddingston near Glasgow, where our father was based at the time. Her mother was living with us and it was there she died. She is buried near Glasgow.

## 2

AFTER OUR PARENTS' MARRIAGE, the family lived for a time at number 15 The Bowling Green, where Brian was born on the 5th of October 1911. He was the third son – a year and a half younger than I and three years younger than Gearóid.

In 1912 my father was transferred to Glasgow. There we lived in Athol Gardens, Sheepburn Road, Uddingston, which is a suburb of Glasgow. The family remained in Scotland for a few years but returned to Ireland before 1916.

Back in Ireland we settled in a terrace of four houses called 'St Michael's' on Sarsfield Road, Inchicore, where a branch of the road (St Laurence's Road) leads down to Chapelizod. The Revenue Commissioners owned this terrace and nobody lived there except Customs & Excise officers. Our father worked in the distillery in Chapelizod.

The terrace of houses in Inchicore is still there but the change in the surrounding countryside is indescribable. In our time there were green fields behind the houses with trees and a stream at the bottom of the fields – it was open country.

Now it is covered in concrete with the buildings of Ballyfermot reaching out to the farthest horizon.

Our neighbours in the adjoining houses of the Inchicore terrace were Mangan, O'Donovan and Morris. We had little contact with the Mangans but were on friendly terms with the other two families. Dermot Morris was about my own age and the four of us – Brian, Gearóid, Dermot and I – used to play together. In later years Dermot became a prominent lawyer and won international recognition as a rugby player at full-back for Ireland.

Brian, Gearóid and I used to play in the fields at the back of the house or occasionally in the front garden. At other times we would simply watch the world go by at the wall overlooking the main road. Once while playing in the fields we found a small bottle half filled with some light-coloured liquid. Brian drank it. On returning home one or other of us mentioned the 'find' to our father, who immediately set about preparing some kind of emetic which he made Brian drink.

Occasionally we would be taken for a walk by the maid – wheeling a pram occupied by the latest addition to the family. We were never without a maid and at one time, I remember, when the family was very big, we had need of two maids. On our walks we would go as far as Kilmainham Gaol or for a couple of miles along the country roads that stretched up to Ballyfermot.

We visited the city often enough – I remember a day when my father took us to see a film in the Sackville Cinema in Lower O'Connell Street. The cinema was almost opposite Daniel O'Connell's statue, on the Post Office side of the street. I remember little about the film except that it was a 'Western' with people shooting one another every few minutes.

Another early memory remains firm – the night my father decided to teach us how to read. He cut a piece of cardboard into little squares and wrote a letter of the alphabet on each one. Then he put them together to form words.

During our time in Inchicore there was some danger after dark on the road from Chapelizod. Father took a heavy stick with him every day, and once. I heard him tell my mother that he had had to walk on top of the wall, part of the way, the previous night! I never discovered what the danger was but I imagine it may have been wild animals.

A visitor who came to our house from time to time and who was always given a great welcome was our Uncle Gearóid. He was about forty years old at that time. He did not arrive as most people did, on foot, but in a car! He must have been one of the first people in Ireland to have a car, if you exclude the real pioneers. Cars were not common in Ireland until 1908 – the year Ford introduced the famous Model T to the market. Indeed it was a Ford that my uncle had but I do not remember much about it except its brass radiator.

Besides having a car, Father Gearóid used to bring a breath of adventure into the house. He was different – he smoked cigarettes, indeed he was a chain-smoker. Our father did not smoke so it was unusual and in some respects pleasant to get the smell of tobacco around the house. Playing tricks with cards was another of his specialities. He had a strange accent on his Irish and on the odd English word, too – 'Bhfuil sibh alright?' (Are you alright?), as we packed ourselves into his car. Down to Maynooth we would go, but not usually to St Patrick's College, though we were there a couple of times. More often than not we went to the Convent of Mercy, where he was on friendly terms with some of the nuns.

When left to our own devices, we spent a lot of time looking over the wall at the end of the garden. There was very little traffic on the roads at that time but you would see the odd interesting thing if you stayed there long enough. A ragged tramp came by now and then. He was a fairly young man with a black beard. 'Blackbird Soup' was the nickname the local boys had for him, a jeering reference to the kind of diet he was supposed to have lived on. They used to call the name after him when he had gone about fifty yards past them. He would chase them, yelling like a madman and they screaming, half terrified he would catch them. In time, instead of chasing them he took to throwing stones.

Another time, when the three of us were at the wall we saw a spectacular sight which made a deep impression on me. It must have been before the Rising that we witnessed this event – a group of boys marching from the direction of Inchicore. They were a group of Irish Volunteers wearing hats and full uniform. There were about sixteen of them and they marched in two columns. They played pipes as they marched past but they had no drum. The spectacle excited me enormously. I could hardly have known who they were but instinctively I sensed that they stood for Ireland and represented bravery and glory. They marched up towards Ballyfermot and were soon out of sight.

I never thought of asking Brian if he remembered the Rising – he would have been about five at the time, and I six and a half. All I saw of the Rising was the redness of the sky from the big fires that were burning in the middle of the city. There must have been a lot of discussion about the Rising in our house, but if I heard it I have long forgotten it. However, I remember our father revealing his attitude a few months afterwards when an English airship came across the sky and flew over our house. 'Where is it going?' I asked him. 'To Hell, I hope,' he answered.

# 3

WE LEFT INCHICORE at the beginning of 1917. Father had been promoted and was now an unattached surveyor. His new responsibilities involved a lot of travelling, and as he would often be away from home he decided to rent a house in Strabane so that my mother could be near her own family. So we resettled in Ballycolman Lane, at the Bridge End of the town. In 1917, apart from the houses at the Bridge End of this narrow road, there were few houses until you reached the top of the road where it joins the road to Omagh. There was an odd large house, a few cottages and a single farm, with the church of Melmont and its graveyard standing sentinel at the top of the road. The scene is very changed today, with houses built the length of the road, a big housing estate and a golf course at the upper end. The name is changed too. It is now 'Ballycolman Avenue' – 'Lane' wasn't swanky enough for the new tenants or for the developers who wished to sell their houses to them.

Our house was quite big. It had two parts – it is likely that it had been extended. The part that fronted the road was single-storey with a thatched roof and consisted of four rooms and a kitchen. The part behind was a two-storey extension. It is difficult to fathom why the extension was carried out in the way that it was. As well as the garden in front and a yard at the back, there was a large orchard that belonged to the house but was not included in the contract as part of our holding. Just as there were fields at the back of our house in Inchicore, we had them here too – acres and acres of them down to the river. There was a private path down through the fields to the river which was a great shortcut to the town.

There was a ghost in the house – a poltergeist. As I cannot make any judgment on the matter I will simply record the facts.

My mother and my sister Róisín, who was about four years old, slept upstairs in the high part of the house. Brian, Gearóid, myself and another brother – that was the extent of the family at that time – slept downstairs in the front part of the house. We heard nothing unusual and were told nothing of the strange events that occurred until long afterwards.

I do not know how soon it was after our arrival that my mother first became aware of the ghost, but it was not long before she asked her sister, our aunt Teresa, to come and sleep in our house. Mother was afraid to be by herself at night without another adult for company. Aunt Teresa would come to our house every night after she closed the shop she managed in Market Street. What form did the haunting take? I simply repeat the story as I often heard it from my mother and my aunt:

You would waken in the darkness, knowing that something had just woken you. You would lie there waiting – full of anticipation. Presently, you would hear the sash of a window being pulled up roughly, even though you knew all the windows were closed and locked. Then the sound of a small iron ball being rolled across the bedroom floor. This would be followed by the sound of something heavy falling down the stairs making massive thumps.

Things used to happen during the day, too. Occasionally if my mother was in the drawing-room she would hear a great commotion coming from the kitchen as though a couple of hens had come indoors and were flying about. On going to the kitchen to investigate she would find nothing. There would be no hens near the door – indeed the door itself would often be closed. On other occasions she would find everything from the mantelpiece in the drawing-room thrown onto the floor.

Aunt Teresa used to come up from town at about eight o'clock. Usually she'd come in the back door. An odd night my mother would hear her step on the gravel at the side of the house but she would not come in. Again, on going to the kitchen, my mother would find nobody there. Half an hour later she would hear the step again and Teresa would appear.

There was a room in the house that was locked – the landlord neither supplied a key nor said why it was locked. It was a small room close to the kitchen, and you could see into it through a window on the outside of the house. The window was high up in the wall and had iron bars on it, as did all the lower windows except for a few at the front of the house. I remember a day – it must have been after a bad night's visitation by the ghost – when my mother took a kitchen chair and stood on it to look into the room. Later, we copied her as children do, without knowing why. I could see nothing through the window other than a piece of shelf and the floor.

Uncle Peter, a Carmelite from Aungier Street in Dublin, visited us and was asked to say Mass in the house. He did and I remember the occasion very well because I had to learn the Latin responses so that I could serve the Mass. The Mass was celebrated in the drawing-room.

There was another odd thing about our haunted house in Strabane. My mother had a clutch of hens with a hen-house near the house itself. Foot nor claw would any of those hens put inside that hen-house. I often tried to coax them into the house with no success – they refused to shelter in it at night. Instead they flew up into the trees at the side of the house and roosted there. Nights of hard frost or strong gales made no difference – they elected to roost in the trees.

# 4

BRIAN WAS TWELVE YEARS OF AGE when he was first sent to school. I was thirteen and a half and my older brother fifteen. Why we were not sent to school earlier is not clear. It may have been due to our not living in one place for more than two or three years, until we finally settled in Dublin in 1923. Róisín, who was younger than Brian, Gearóid or myself, was sent to school while we lived in Tullamore; we were not. It has been suggested that our father feared that school, as it was then, would weaken our Irish, but I find that hard to believe. While we never spoke anything but Irish amongst ourselves, we had as much English as any other children. This was due to the fact that my mother's family spoke only English and it was seldom that one or another of them was not visiting us. Aunt Teresa, who had no Irish, slept in our house every night because of the ghost, and hardly a day passed when we were not in their house in the Main Street or in one of the shops – places where only English was spoken.

Since we were attending no school and our father was away

from home a lot of the time, a difficulty arose about being taught catechism so that we could be confirmed. One of the McDevitt family, who had a draper's shop in Abercorn Square, came to the rescue. Sometimes he would come to our house and instruct us or we would go to the McDevitt family home near the top of Ballycolman Lane.

It was in the Melmont church at the top of Ballycolman Lane that we received communion and were confirmed. I remember being quite anxious that morning. I had been told that it was part of the ceremony for the bishop to give a blow to each child as a sign of something or other in the Christian life. It would be an exaggeration to suggest that I was expecting a knock-out blow, but I did anticipate a hard blow, especially if I failed to produce prompt answers to the bishop's questions. I was mightily relieved when I saw that the bishop was only giving a pat on the cheek to the boys in front of me.

During the Strabane years, efforts were made to have us taught at home. A girl called O'Boyle was our first teacher. After that we had a school-teacher named Collins. My memory of him is his reading J.P. Craig's version of *Clann Lir*, which was in Ulster Irish. After Mr Collins stopped coming, our father tried teaching us by post, writing from wherever in Ireland his business had taken him, setting out lessons to be done. It is likely that we did not do these lessons or did them so badly that the experiment was abandoned.

Whatever teaching or lack of it we were given at home in Strabane or later in Tullamore, one thing is certain – it had no adverse effect on us. During the day we were free to do as we pleased. Nor does this freedom appear to have done us any harm. It is a subject that has never been properly examined – assuming that parents had a plentiful supply of books covering a wide range of subjects and the children were seen to be reading, then maybe it would be better to keep them from school until they were in their teens.

On the other hand, had we been at school when young we would have been socializing with children of our own age. As matters stood no encouragement was given to mix with the children of the neighbourhood, though we were not expressly forbidden to do so. Instead, we became so numerous as a family – there were twelve of us eventually – that we had sufficient company amongst ourselves. In the end it is likely a bad thing to grow up without socializing widely with other children.

I remember one occasion when we were playing football in the road with the children who lived at the bottom of Ballycolman Lane. We used a paper ball, which was made by rolling a lot of pieces of paper and pressing them very tightly together and tying the bundle with twine. Nowadays, when even the poorest travelling people would have a proper ball, people find it very hard to understand how scarce basic items were in the 1920s. Nor would they recognize the great variety of goods that have become available because of the progress in manufacturing and the invention of new materials such as plastic.

The house in Ballycolman Lane was a strange house, quite apart from having a resident ghost. There was a passage that gave access from the front of the house to the back. A door in the middle of this passage led into a laundry. This room was fully equipped for washing, with an abundant supply of water and outlets in the concrete floor for drainage. Above the laundry there was another room, which had stone steps leading to it from the outside, totally separate from the rest of the house. This room was used as a store-room and it was here that we spent a lot of our time.

We were smoking brown-paper cigarettes then and it was essential to be in a secure place where our mother could not come upon us suddenly. There were hundreds of Gaelic League booklets belonging to our father stored in this room. He had used and distributed them in the Irish classes he had taught in Strabane prior to his marriage. These yellow-covered booklets (*Tá na Francaigh ar Muir*, a play by Cú Uladh, *Prátaí Mhíchel Thaidhg*, etc.) were tied in bundles with wrapping paper and twine. One day I noticed the wrapping paper and it struck me that it might make good cigarette paper. It was soft, dark grey, half-rotten paper with mildew on it and it tore very easily. I should explain that an essential quality demanded of brown paper for cigarette-making is that it should smoulder away without going out or having to be continually drawn to keep it alight. Test results proved excellent – this dark grey paper lit up at once, burned strongly and gave out thick, light grey smoke. Indeed, it was too good in some ways for it was difficult to extinguish quickly whenever grown-ups came near our loft. If the least spark remained, it would rekindle, until all the paper glowed red again.

We smoked this paper for as long as it lasted. There must have been a terrible smell from the smoke but to us it was a fragrant aroma. In comparison to ordinary brown paper, it seemed to us akin to Turkish tobacco! We were devastated when the last of it was smoked. We searched the house from top to bottom looking for more of it but never found such tasty paper as the Gaelic League used for wrapping their booklets. Maybe it is just as well – God knows what cancer or other terrible disease would have afflicted anyone who kept smoking it.

At that time we had a sharp eye for brown paper. When a parcel was being unwrapped in the house, we would be looking at the brown paper, assessing its suitability for making cigarettes. There was no better judge of brown paper in Ireland at that time than I, even if I say so myself. I would know at a glance whether it would light up well and continue burning – that insight is with me still! Brown paper, for example, that has a shiny finish is the very worst for cigarettes. There is no use even trying it – it won't light up and the devil himself couldn't keep it going.

# 5

DURING THE SUMMER we spent a lot of time at the river-side. Wading about in the water, with our boots tied together by the laces and slung around our necks, was a favourite pastime. I do not remember what we were doing – we certainly were not fishing; that activity came into its own only when the river was in flood. In any event we became very knowledgable about that stretch of the river near the town. We could pinpoint every hole and underwater rock and the likely locations of a resting trout or a coiled eel.

On other days we would go up the river bank as far as Camas where the water is dark and deep even in summer. Seven fields up the bank of the river there was a chance you would see a seal, and there would be hundreds of swallows skimming and diving when the midges appeared in the sunlight.

These were stirring times in the political life of the country – war and unrest were in the air. Nevertheless, if I had to choose the quietest, happiest days I can remember in my whole life, I would pick the years 1917 to 1920. I remember especially long summer days when we would be lying on the high grassy banks at the riverside. Days when you could imagine that the sun was standing in the sky – with time suspended – no movement except for the river and no sound except the hum of insects and the far-away throb of the shirt factory giving out the pulse of summer.

The river was only one aspect of our lives in Strabane. Apart from our life at home, the rapport we had with my mother's family influenced us enormously.

As I've already said, my mother's father was John Gormley. His father before him was a shopkeeper. My mother's mother was from the MacLoinsigh family. Her father, Liam MacLoinsigh, was a miller in Clare, near Castle Derg in County Tyrone. The walls of Clare Mill are still standing but the water-wheel has not survived.

Just as there are twelve in our family, there were twelve Gormleys, but five of them died in childhood. The Gormleys, in order of birth, were: Teresa, Mary Louise (died in infancy), Jack, William (died in infancy), Agnes (my mother), Thomas (died in infancy), Thomas, Edmund (died in infancy), Mary Josephine (died aged six), Eugene, George and Joseph.

Only Teresa, Eugene and Thomas are alive today [1973]. As for the others, Joseph died in 1969; and there wouldn't be a middle-aged journalist in Dublin who would not remember George Gormley, who died in the mid-sixties. He spent his life working in the Dublin newspapers, most of it with the *Irish Independent*.

As children we were aware of the unrest and excitement that was all around us during those years, although we did not understand it. England was threatening to conscript the Irish into her army and send them to France. It is unlikely that there was a town in Ireland where active opposition to this threat was not being organized. My aunt Teresa and her friends from Cumann na mBan used to meet in a hall in Barrack Street where public meetings, concerts and *céilithe* were held to raise money. I remember being at a *céile* in the Town Hall and looking down at the dancers from the gallery. It was exciting and somewhat special for me to be out so late at night. Against this glamour of an evening *céile* something ominous was happening – young men were drilling.

Uncle Eugene was the first to start organizing opposition to conscription. In 1918 he was arrested, brought by train to Belfast and marched between two policemen from Edward Street Station to Victoria Military Barracks. A contingent of soldiers from the Northumbria Fusiliers accompanied them. Belfast people must have wondered at this young man who was being escorted through the streets with such a strong guard – who was he and what had he done? My uncle thinks it was simply a coincidence that the soldiers were returning to barracks at the same time.

Trial by military court quickly followed. A soldier who escorted him to court advised, out of the corner of his mouth, 'Don't let those f—ing bastards send you to jail – recognize the court.' Refusing to recognize the court, he was sentenced to six months in Crumlin Road Jail. Ernest Blythe and Austin Stack were fellow prisoners. Uncle Eugene was arrested again in 1922 and imprisoned on the *Argenta*, where the other prisoners elected him as their leader. Cahir Healy was among those held on the prison ship. Eugene was never a member of the IRA.

In 1918 a virulent flu spread across Europe – it killed more people than had lost their lives in the war. It was like the nameless plagues that have followed wars from times immemorial. I was the only one in our house to catch a dose of this flu and I believe it was the most serious illness I've ever had – I was in bed for three weeks.

Our father came home at weekends whenever he was within reasonable travelling distance. On one of these occasions he took us on a walk to Victoria Bridge and we came home by train. Another time he took us to the top of Knockavoe, the mountain overlooking Strabane, and we gathered mulberries.

Brian Gearóid and I visited Maggie Payne, a native Irish-speaker from Donegal. Maggie was an old woman at the time and lived in a little house a short distance out the Derry Road. Our exchanges with her were in Irish, of course.

Another day we were at a farm on the 'threshing' day. The farm was only a quarter of a mile from our house in Ballycolman Lane. Today you would need to explain to young people what used to happen on threshing day. On an arranged day at harvest time the threshing machine would arrive, pulled by a steam engine that was not unlike a railway engine. This machinery and many willing hands were there for the full day to thresh all the grain that the farmer had, which would be standing ready in stooks. There is no describing the excitement, fun and noise of that day. I was lucky to catch a glimpse of a field mouse escaping through the stubble.

That autumn Brian went into McAleer's shoemaking shop at the Bridge End and asked for work. Mr McAleer assented and said he could start the next morning. Of course, my mother did not let him out next morning – he was about eight years of age at the time!

# 6

THE TWO SHOPS that my mother's family had in Strabane have now been sold and trade under new names. The shop and dwelling-house in the Main Street was a second home to us as long as the Gormleys were there, not just when we were young and living locally but long afterwards.

The house was a big one with lots of bedrooms, so there was no difficulty in accommodating four or five visitors at a time. When we were at school in Dublin and later at university, hardly a year passed but we were in Strabane for a holiday, spending weeks or even a month there. When going to the Donegal Gaeltacht we did not have to make the journey in one day, as most people did, but could break the journey by staying a day or two in Strabane.

It was natural for children to find fascination in the shops and to spend a lot of time in them, reading comics and magazines and listening to the talk of the town. In those days people had time to stand and exchange news and stories from far and near. People came into town from Castle Derg, from

Gurteen, from the Sperrins and Dunmanway, Bridgetown and Castlefin. It must be remembered that the cursed border did not exist in those halcyon days. The people of south-east Donegal did their shopping in Strabane but the border signalled the ruination of the town's commercial base.

I remember the fairs in Strabane before the establishment of the border – the streets would be so crowded that you could walk across the street on people's heads! Below in Abercorn Square, youths would be standing, waiting for some farmer to hire them – these were the hiring fairs so well documented in the stories of Séamus Ó Grianna, Peadar O'Donnell and others.

At the back of the Gormley house there was a large yard containing two or three granite buildings where all kinds of merchandise for the shops was stored. Delph, china, toys, novelties, leather goods and ornaments were laid out on shelves or held in packing cases. It would be hard to find or imagine a better place for children to play – free as we were from the foolish slavery of school! As an alternative to the stores we could go upstairs in the house itself to the sitting-room, where there was a piano, a gramophone and lots of records. This room had an excellent view of the Main Street and all that was happening there from its three lofty windows.

There was talent for music in both our mother's and father's families. Our uncle Joe Gormley organized concerts, operas and stage productions in the town. He trained both choirs and soloists. Some of his songs were broadcast on Radio Éireann and a few were recorded.

In the time I am recalling (1917–20), Joe Gormley was mainly obsessed with drama. While we were still living in Inchicore he had stayed with us for a time while serving his apprenticeship to photography with one of the big companies in Dublin. His father had arranged this training course for him, and when he returned to Strabane a shop fitted out with cameras and other equipment was rented for him in Market Street. By the time we came to the town he had opened his photographer's shop, but it did not prove to be a good business prospect – there were already two such shops in the town with scarcely room for a third. Had Joe been a go-getter in the American style he might have succeeded, but he was not that kind of person.

The floor over the shop, though equipped for the processing of films, became a rehearsal studio for a play that was to be staged in the Town Hall. A group of boys and girls were assembled, with my uncles George and Joe coaching them. Those taking part got great fun out of their roles and we enjoyed watching the direction they were being given. The play was called *Tactics*.

I began to learn the harp in 1919. We had a harp in the house which had been made by a famous harp-maker in Belfast – it had been a wedding present to my father. I did not continue the lessons for very long – I thought that the harmony was too thin. Nor did I like pulling at the strings with cold fingers on bleak winter mornings in the teacher's room. Instead I began learning the piano and I did not abandon this instrument until forced to as a result of an accident in 1952.

Brian studied the violin, but he did not begin until we were settled in Dublin in 1923.

In July 1920 the landlord gave us notice to quit the house in Ballycolman Lane. The notice shows that the rent we were paying was £7-10-0 per quarter. In the event my father did not care – the Commissioners had just transferred him as a permanent surveyor to Tullamore. It was to that town that we moved towards the end of the year 1920.

# 7

CAPPENCUR WAS THE NAME of the district in Tullamore where we lived from November 1920 until the summer of 1923. Cappencur is about two miles outside the town on the Daingean road. At that time Daingean was more often referred to as Philipstown. In our time there was only our house, Daly's farmhouse and three or four small houses farther down the road in Cappencur; now it boasts a factory. The two miles of road into Tullamore was as straight as a rush – you could even see some of the town's buildings indistinctly from our gate. Travelling from Tullamore I do not remember any other houses on that road until you reached our house. That house, which is still there but greatly changed, is on the right-hand side of the road. It was called 'The Copper Beeches', an apt name as the avenue leading up to the house was lined with big, majestic, red-leafed beech trees. A spacious lawn in front of the house hosted a weeping willow and flowering shrubs. The house had a garden and a large orchard on one side with a smaller garden on the other. There was a large farmyard at the back which included a hay-shed, stables and other outhouses with a lane at the side for carts. 'The Beeches' was rented from the Odlums.

It was dark when we arrived at 'The Beeches' on that first night in November. There was a huge blazing fire on a big, wide hearth to greet us – a turf fire. We were, of course, right in the heart of turf country.

One of the first things our father did when we had settled in Tullamore was to buy a car. A car was necessary as his work took him to places like Kilbeggan (Locke's Distillery) and Edenderry. The make of car he chose was the Overland. One of his duties was to visit farmers all over the county who were growing tobacco. He often took all three of us. I remember visiting Birr. Another time it was the nursery in Geashil, where seeds and plants were purchased. Brian mentions Geashil a couple of times in his writings – it must have been this trip which left the name in his memory.

I will not attempt to describe the Overland. But if the difference between the car of the twenties and that of today is great, the change that has taken place on the roads during the same period is equally dramatic. An uncle of mine held the view that the greatest revolution of the first half of the century was the macadam method of road-making. In 1920 and for years afterwards every road in the country was a kind of 'dirt' road. There are a great number of words in Irish for mud – *clábar, lábán* or *láib, lathach, draoib, puiteach, greallach.* Perhaps there was a need for all of them at one time but there is scarcely any need for even one of them today, for mud has largely been banished from the roads. At that time if you looked along a stretch of road on a wet day, it would seem as if there were scores of basins of water laid out as far as the eye could see. These were round holes filled with rain-water, pot-holes they were called, and the surface in between was covered in a thick skin of mud.

While the roads were muddy and dirty on wet days, they were no better on dry summer days. Every car or lorry that passed raised a cloud of dust that would smother you. The dust was so thick that the vehicle raising it would disappear in a cloud. Experience taught you to have your eyes half closed to keep the dust from blinding you.

The Overland had to be washed on Saturday, and father would bring it to the farmyard where there was a large trough of water and a water pump. After its week's work on mud roads it was sorely in need of a wash and we had to lend a helping hand.

During the early twenties the motor-car was not the usual mode of transport in Offaly. Getting from place to place was more commonly done by donkey and cart or by pony and trap. You could hardly come across a stretch of road without three or four donkeys and carts carrying their loads of turf. And at harvest time there were queues of these carts carrying turf everywhere you went with the driver sitting on the shaft, or, if the cart was empty, the driver standing on it doing great feats of balancing as the donkey trotted.

On Sunday the two miles of road into Tullamore was thronged with people going to Mass – in donkey carts, in traps and on bicycles – with the odd motor-car.

The bicycle was very popular in the country in the twenties. There can scarcely have been a farmer who did not have one, even if he had a pony and trap as well. The traffic on the road to Mass would include scores of bicycles, with straight-backed farmers dressed up in their blue suits. Many of these bicycles were of Irish manufacture – Pierce or Lucanta; they seemed like tanks compared with bicycles of other makes because of their weight and the thickness of their frames.

In those days an elderly person or even a middle-aged man would never dream of mounting a bicycle by throwing his leg over the saddle as a younger person would. Instead he would use the 'back-step', as it was called – a steel bar about three inches long that extended from the hub of the back wheel on the left-hand side. To mount the bicycle using the 'back-step' you took a firm grip of the handlebars, stretched your body back so that your legs were to the rear of the bicycle and you began to run, pushing the bicycle in front of you. When you had achieved sufficient speed you stepped onto the 'back-step' and let yourself down into the saddle. There is no 'back-step' on bicycles now so that method of mounting will never be seen again.

There are some things in life that can only be learned by taking a chance: swimming is one of these, cycling another. I remember seeing an example of this when visiting a friend's house. A middle-aged woman, who had bought herself a new bicycle, was sitting on it 'learning' to ride. Casual observation suggested that she would never succeed in doing so. Another woman was walking beside the bicycle lending support and bearing most of the learner's weight on her shoulder. Whenever the bicycle was straightened the learner would become terrified and give a little scream. That was the sign for the instructor to take charge and restore the equilibrium. They went up and down the yard three or four times while I was there and for all the progress they made it might as well have been a sack of potatoes that was on the bicycle!

Early in 1921, before Lloyd George's offer to de Valera in June of that year, the fight for freedom was at its fiercest and we knew all about it in Tullamore. The Black and Tan lorries often flashed past our house at great speed. Those rascals always sat back-to-back facing outwards with their guns on their knees. One evening when we were having dinner, one of the lorries stopped directly outside our house and a couple of men got out and began to lift stones from the low boundary wall between our lawn and the road. One of us asked our father, 'Why should we let them do that?' He answered that it did not matter and that we would not dispute the territory with them at that time.

When travelling with our father in the car we often met Black and Tan lorries, and wisdom dictated that one drew into the side of the road to let them pass as they never reduced their speed. At the time you would never travel far on a main road without encountering a bridge over a river or canal that had not been blown up overnight. Temporary repairs would be in place to give you access but there would always be officers and soldiers there to question you.

During that time I remember lying awake at night and hearing the sound of trees being cut down by volunteers so that they would block the road between Daingean and Tullamore.

The soldiers came to our house on two occasions. The first time was at night shortly after our arrival in Tullamore. I do not know what they wanted, but when they were leaving they took away a sword belonging to the Odlum family which was hanging in the hall as an ornament. On the second occasion they were looking for help to clear a tree that had been knocked down near the house. This was a ploy to gather men and force them to do the clearance work.

# 8

AS FAR AS I KNOW, Brian did no creative writing until he was in his last year in Blackrock College. Even then the extent of his output was a few short poems. I myself began to write, if it is correct to use such a sophisticated word for it, when we were still living in Tullamore. I would walk into the town to buy notebooks as I believed that my work needed to be set formally in book form as distinct from loose pages. I used to fill these notebooks with novels, which no doubt were pure rubbish.

One of the 'novels' went to a great friend of my mother – a Mrs Mary Gallagher, who was a widow living in Strabane at the time. Mary Gallagher was very involved in the nationalist movement and as a consequence her house was raided by the police. The house was ransacked from top to bottom in the hope of finding treasonable documents. The police found nothing of that kind but they did come across this 'book' of mine. They did not understand it, good, bad or indifferent! Not surprisingly, they thought that they had stumbled upon something important. Subsequent intense questioning of Mrs Gallagher could elicit no satisfactory answers!

Although Brian was not writing at that time it's likely he was reading avidly. By then I had read everything in the house. The collection of books my father had was not very large but it was broad and varied. The Public Library system had not yet been established nor was there any talk of such a venture. People who wished to have books had to buy them, and there were no cheap paperback editions. My father was a regular buyer of books – I remember, while living in Inchicore in 1916, him arriving home with a copy of the first edition of O'Corcora's *A Munster Twilight*.

Thomas Hardy and Joseph Conrad were two authors that my father liked particularly, and he bought all of their books. I cannot recall the other authors that appealed to him, but he had most of Robert Louis Stevenson's, even those that you seldom see, such as *Across the Plains*, *The Silverado Squatters* and, of course, books like *The Wrong Box* which Stevenson wrote in co-operation with Lloyd Osbourne. When I was very young I was given *Treasure Island* as a birthday present. What a pity reading Stevenson went out of fashion – he was a great writer and no doubt he will be rediscovered.

Strange to say we had no Dickens except for *The Pickwick Papers*, although we had all his works at a later date in Dublin. Among other novelists and writers whose work was in the house were the Brontë sisters, Trollope (*Autobiography*), George Eliot, Defoe, George A. Birmingham (*The Northern Iron*), George Meredith, Arthur Conan Doyle, H.G. Wells, Ambrose Bierce, Arnold Bennett, James Stephens, Jane Austen, Nathaniel Hawthorne's *The House of the Seven Gables* – one of the most difficult books to read. There were many other less well-known authors whose names I have forgotten. Among the books other than novels were all the plays of Shakespeare (the Windsor Shakespeare), collections of poems of the principal poets in English, *The Faerie Queene* (Book I), the essays of Dryden, and Hazlitt's essays. We had Mangan and Ferguson among the Anglo-Irish poets; *The Literary History of Ireland* by Douglas Hyde; and that work which is symptomatic of that period – the six volumes of D'Alton's *History of Ireland* in their green covers. *The Life of Gladstone* by Morley and *The Origin of Species* were in the house. I tried to read and understand Darwin's book but failed. There were many Greek and Latin books including all Cicero's letters *Ad Atticium*.

We had few Irish books in Tullamore as they simply were not available. Although Pádraic Ó Conaire began to write as early as 1906, the majority of his best books, including *Seacht mBua an Éirí Amach*, did not appear until 1918. The collection of Irish books that we did have in Tullamore included a good anthology by Flanagan, *Tóraíocht Dhiarmada agus Ghráinne* (The Pursuit of Diarmuid and Gráinne), and the poems of Dháibhí Uí Bhruadair. There were others such as *Seachrán Chairn tSiail, Brisleach Mhór Mhaighe Muirtheimhne, Amhráin Ghrá Chúige Chonnacht* and a handful of others – none of which would inspire a person to write. Had Brian been prompted to write in those days it is likely that it would have been in English. My attempts were also in English for the simple reason that the books which inspired or provoked me to write were all written in English. Proof that even a native speaker like Seosamh Mac Grianna was forced to adopt the language of the majority comes from his own words:

When I was fourteen I wrote a story about the Great War, a book of about 7000 words. Most of what I wrote from that time until I was nineteen was in English. But then I came across *An Chéad Chloch agus Aistí Eile* by Pádraic Ó Conaire.

After Mass on Sunday we usually went to a convent in Tullamore where the nuns ran a small library. The selection of books included the novels of Sabatini and Stacpoole, George Birmingham's *Spanish Gold*, Conan Doyle and many more of that kind. We took a few books home each week, so we were never short of reading matter – but it was always in English.

If Brian was not interested in writing during our time in Tullamore, he was preoccupied with another form of composition – making films. In those days the 'silent' films were captivating the public at large. I do not remember where the picture house in Tullamore was located – it was just an ordinary hall adapted, using heavy blinds on its windows. There was a show in this picture house once a week and the three of us, Gearóid, Brian and I, would walk into town to the show whenever we were allowed. It is hardly surprising that the 'pictures' excited and provoked us – we wanted to have films of our own, at home! Had we had a magic lantern we might have been satisfied. However, there was no prospect of acquiring such equipment because as children we did not have pocket money. In the end we succeeded in founding our own 'film industry', and industry it certainly was, considering all the toil, work and tears that were needed to keep it going!

It started when we found a large lens somewhere in the house. We knew that if you place a lamp behind the lens and put a slide or film the right distance from it, it will project an image onto a screen. So we had the equipment for projecting pictures. But first, all these elements – lens, lamp and a frame to carry the film – had to be contained in a box. This did not present any great difficulty. Being ambitious, we wanted to show 'films' of our own creation: paper strips, one and a quarter inches in depth (the size that suited the lens), that would have pictures drawn on them with ink. These pictures would be telling a story which would be accompanied by a commentary explaining what the characters were saying, as in real films. Ideally, there would be sufficient pictures to keep the 'film' going for a quarter of an hour.

Difficulties beset any enterprise and have to be met with all kinds of solutions. Paper is not transparent no matter how heavily it is inked, especially when the only source of light is an oil lamp! Those were some of the great problems that beset the film industry in 'The Beeches', Cappencur, in the year 1922.

Hollywood experienced similar difficulties with the density of the film material in the early years. As a consequence Hollywood did not really progress until the new film material, which has been in use ever since, was invented.

Whatever solutions Hollywood achieved in improving film quality it can hardly have been as simple and inexpensive as our own invention. I do not remember which of us tumbled to it, but all you had to do was let a tiny drop of paraffin down onto the paper. The paraffin spread evenly all over the paper and left it almost as transparent as film or slide, without affecting the blackness of the ink images. Of course, there was always a very unpleasant smell from the paraffin-soaked paper, but that didn't cost you a thought if you were a real cinema enthusiast!

God be with the foolishness of youth. Brian and I spent whole days bent over tables drawing pictures on strips of paper. He would make one film, I another. Once that had been done, the picture house, which was in the garage, had to be set up – with chairs brought out from the house and posters advertising the show put up. After all that, you had to try to persuade the grown-ups to come and see the show! I regret to admit that this was no easy task — they were reluctant to interrupt whatever they were doing and worse still some were very slow to pay at the door!

When I think now of all that wasted time, the childishness, I wonder at our naïvety. On second thoughts it may be that it was a better way of passing the time than learning about drugs — a real danger for twelve-year-old children today.

# 9

OCCASIONALLY OUR FATHER'S BUSINESS took him to
Dublin for a couple of days. For such trips he would travel by
train. On one of these trips he took Brian and me to the railway station in a taxi. On the return journey we decided that it
would be opportune, in his absence, to launch a boat that I
had made. My interest in boats and indeed in having one of my
own arose from watching the boats that carried turf on the
Grand Canal. Nobody in their senses, other than myself,
would recognize the 'boat' I had assembled. In reality it was
only the framework of an old, discarded pram that had pieces
of wood nailed to it. Undaunted, we carried the 'boat' to a
deep pool in the corner of a field. We lowered it carefully onto
the water, an exercise that was far from easy as there were
steep banks with the water a couple of feet below. The 'boat'
remained on the surface of the water for about five seconds,
then it sank slowly to the bottom. Had it floated for a few minutes it is almost certain that one or other of us would have
gone on board – and at the time neither of us could swim.

Summer evenings in Tullamore were often devoted to croquet. We all played – our father, Gearóid, Brian, Róisín, Fergus and I – on the spacious lawn at the front of the house. Our father had bought the croquet set, a good hickory one, at an auction. Anyone who has played the game will know that there is a lot more to it than driving the ball through a series of iron hoops. It is superior to pitch and putt because the rules allow you, indeed encourage you, to upset your opponents and deflect them from achieving their objectives.

Should you succeed in making a cannon on another ball, one which is perhaps positioned to go through a hoop, you earn an extra shot. Before taking this extra shot you are allowed to reposition your own ball in the most advantageous position, providing it remains in contact with the other player's ball. The outcome, if you play this properly, will ensure that your ball goes where you wish, perhaps through a hoop, and simultaneously your opponent's ball is driven off the pitch or maybe off the lawn altogether if your shot is sufficiently strong. This will ensure that your opponent will not be able to go through a hoop as he intended but may need two shots to get back into place again.

I relate all this detail because it impinges on an incident in one of our many games. Although it is fifty years since it happened, one particular game is as vivid in my memory as if it were only yesterday. Brian cannoned our father's ball just as he was positioned to go through the last hoop and win. When he was fixing his ball behind father's ball to drive him off course I could feel a certain tension. 'Well, he won't give me too hard a blow' or 'He won't drive me too far off course' – these may have been father's sentiments, and while no word was spoken I am certain that Brian felt it just as I did. Brian swung the mallet and struck such a ferocious blow that father's ball was driven across the lawn and out of sight into nearby shrubbery. He must have put all his strength into that blow as he was only eleven at the time. That was his answer to any hopes for softness or favours. He was revealing a strong independent tendency in his nature that was to be recognized later in his writing and in other ways too.

The orchard at the side of the house in Tullamore was full of apple trees – 'eating-apple' trees. The harvest produced so many that we could neither eat them all nor sell them. The odd person who came looking for apples was given all he could carry.

Beside the orchard was the big farmyard behind the house with its stables and outhouses. Some of these buildings were pressed into service, as we had a lot of hens, nine or ten ducks and a single turkey. One great loss for children growing up is to be deprived of seeing one of nature's most emotive sights – the clucking hen and her newly hatched chicks. An insight into animal behaviour, particularly motherhood, is full of wonder and tenderness. In displaying these characteristics the hen surpasses all others in the animal kingdom. Our Lord, when he made his lament over Jerusalem (Luke 13), acknowledged it: 'How often have I longed to gather your children, as a hen gathers her brood under her wing and you would not.' When the hen sits to gather her chicks she spreads out her feathers, increasing her size threefold. Then all the children go inside, as if bidden by some instruction. Shortly afterwards there will always be one or two chicks that put their heads out, one in the hen's breast, another high on the hen's back – like a person looking out of an upstairs window before going to bed!

We had many kinds of hen in Tullamore – black, white and

red. The red ones were big and if they were not already part of the holding when we arrived, we may have acquired them from a neighbouring farm. They were probably of the Rhode Island Red breed originally but there was some cross-breeding with gaming birds in them. This was evident in the ferocity of the fights between the cocks. They would fight until exhausted and covered in blood. If separated, they would simply start again in another corner of the farmyard. Nor were they slow to engage in combat with humans! If you stooped down and flicked your hand near the beak of one of these cocks you would get a quick reaction – the feathers of his hackles rising. He would start cackling angrily and busy himself picking little grains from the ground to put you off your guard; next thing he would launch an aerial attack with a burst of red wings and claws, striking blows around your head. Retreat from this onslaught was always the wisest course.

One year we set duck eggs under a clucking hen. Soon after the ducklings were hatched we made a little pond near the pump in the yard. Imagine the scene when the little ducklings were naturally attracted to the water and began swimming and diving. The concern and consternation of the poor mother hen would bring a smile to the dourest face as she ran around the pond bidding her chicks to come out of the water. Needless to say, the ducklings paid no heed to her pleadings.

When the ducks had grown up they preferred to go a long way down the fields to a nearby stream. They came home in the evening stretched out in single file, with the drake at the head of the line. One could hear this homeward-bound party cackling loudly long before it came into sight.

There was a fat donkey with a gentle, kindly face attached to the farm – it probably belonged to the Odlums. Our immediate reaction on seeing it was that we could have great sport riding the donkey hither and thither. The kindly-faced donkey had other ideas. As soon as I mounted his back he set off at a half-trot towards the nearest wall. I would be a one-legged man today had I not jumped clear in time. We tried to secure his co-operation in other ways but he would always head for the nearest wall. He was left to graze in peace after that.

Another activity of ours during our time in Tullamore was 'building' houses. These shelters in the garden enabled us to be out of doors during showery weather. I had my house in my own private garden and Brian had his nearby. Our father had given each of us a little plot of the garden, hoping to arouse an interest in gardening, which was of special interest to him. My house was built against the garden wall and its walls were made of sacks. The 'house' was hardly big enough to accommodate me when I was sitting down inside it. I remember a day in 1921 when I was inside my house and English soldiers appeared in the garden. They were looking for men to cut and clear a big tree that was blocking the road in front of their lorries. One soldier, rifle at the ready, came down the garden to see if there was anyone about – I watched him come and go, but he didn't see me!

# 10

IN 1923 MY FATHER WAS PROMOTED and transferred to Dublin. We left Tullamore sometime in April or May of that year and moved to a house in Herbert Place. The house is on a stretch of road that runs along the Grand Canal between Mount Street Bridge and Baggot Street Bridge. Most of the houses are now in flats or offices but in those days they were family homes. We lived in number 25, a five-storied house, which our father rented for £90 a year. Large as we were as a family, the house was too big for us, and we made little use of the top floor.

Before dealing with the tremendous change that the move to Dublin made to the lives of Gearóid, Brian and myself, I want to draw a portrait of my father. He was six foot high, strong and active. Although he put on some weight towards the end of his life, he was never fat. He was bald from an early age. Gardening and walking were his favourite exercises. In our view, because he had us as helpers, his methods of preparing soil were excessively laborious. When breaking new ground, or re-digging ground that had become compacted, he insisted on a procedure that the gardening books call 'trenching'. It is simple for me to explain it, considering the number of times we were required to undertake this Herculean task! Having marked out the plot to be 'trenched', you make a deep trench right down to the yellow clay and you transfer the earth by wheelbarrow to the far end of the plot where you intend to finish. Next you begin to fill the trench you have just made by digging and shovelling the ground beside it, always going down to the yellow clay. In a sense you are making new trenches all the time until you reach the end of the plot and you fill the last one with the earth that was taken from the first. Manure would be added throughout the trenching exercise. I think it would have been sufficient to loosen the soil with a fork and spread manure through it. Another habit of our father's was to take every stone, big or small, out of the ground. I have heard it argued that stones are necessary to let the air through the soil and that they should not be removed. It probably depends on whether the soil is heavy or light.

With all this activity in our gardens we always had plenty of potatoes and every vegetable that a housewife could wish for: cabbage of every kind, peas, two kinds of beans, onions, lettuce, turnips, celery, leeks, parsnips, spinach … everything except carrots, which did not grow well because of some fly or other disease. Herbert Place was the only house where we had no garden, but we had a big garden again when we moved out to Blackrock in 1927.

Strangely enough, when our father died I began to do a lot of the work he used to do around the garden as well as cutting turf in the Dublin mountains during the war – proof indeed that necessity is the mother of invention.

If we were raised with Irish, we were also raised with chess.

Our father was a great chess player and all the boys of the family learned the game from an early age. This made most of us strong players in later years.

At university I joined the chess club. It was run by Jimmy, a brother of Roger McHugh. Our father was a member of the Blackrock Chess Club and the Dublin Chess Club. He played regularly in the inter-club competitions. I too played in the competitions until one day the thought struck me that it was madness to spend so much time moving little pieces of wood around a board! I gave it up and have scarcely laid a finger on a chess piece since.

However, father kept up a keen interest in the game, and went to Blackrock College once or twice a week to give lessons to the pupils. I remember coming home one night to find both the sitting-room and the dining-room full of strangers, sitting in pairs playing chess, in a dense cloud of tobacco smoke. Apparently, a visiting chess team had come to Blackrock Library, where the local host team played, to find that the room was unavailable. To remedy the situation our father had asked them to come up to our house.

Early in the thirties one of the famous chess masters, Koltanowski, came to Dublin accompanied by his wife. He must have liked Dublin and the people he met for he stayed six months. Despite his Russian-sounding name he was a Belgian and was world champion in the blindfold simultaneous competition, and as far as I know nobody has taken that title from him. As recently as 1960, if newspaper reports are accurate, he played blind (without sight of any of the boards) against 56 of the best players in San Francisco in an event staged in the Fairmount Hotel. He won 50 of the games and the remaining six were drawn. Koltanowski was in our house a few times, socially and to play chess with our father. He was also in the house of another of our friends, Oscar Quigley. Oscar was a first-class player and at the time published a chess magazine for which Koltanowski wrote a few articles. Koltanowski is supposed to have had a chess school in Sandymount during his stay in Dublin. Brian boasted that he had succeeded in beating him in a game, but I do not believe that.

In April 1925 our father was appointed a Commissioner on the Board of the Revenue Commissioners, which meant that he had attained the highest office in that department of the civil service. He was fifty years of age.

From the evidence available it is clear that our father was an able, intelligent man. He was conscientious in his work and the progress of his career as befitted the head of a family with so many children. However, he was also a man of many interests. He was fond of music and drama. When he was young he made several attempts at writing plays – the manuscripts were uncovered among his papers after he died. He also sent a novel to a London publisher but his literary agent in that city advised against accepting the offer that was made. A one-act play by his brother Fergus Ó Nualláin, entitled *A Royal Alliance,* was staged by the Abbey Theatre in 1920. F.J. McCormick, Barry Fitzgerald, Maureen Delaney and Kathleen Fortune were in the cast. The same brother and our father were supposed to be engaged in some literary project but I don't think anything came of it.

Our father and mother went regularly to plays at the Abbey and Gate theatres. London productions were frequently staged in Dublin and these would be included in our parents' schedule. We children were also taken to the theatre – we saw almost every production of *An Comhar Drámíochta*. We saw the first production in Dublin of *Tóraíocht Dhiarmada agus Ghráinne* by Mícheál Mac Liammóir, with Mac Liammóir himself in the leading role. We went to a lot of English plays too. *Fáinne an Lae, The Irish Statesman* (Æ's paper) and *John O'London's Weekly* were publications to which our father subscribed.

Our house was never without a gramophone and our father was a regular buyer of records. Classical and operatic music were his favourites and our record collection reflected that. We were regular concert-goers, too – especially those given by the Army Band under Colonel Fritz Brase. On Saturdays during the season there were Celebrity Concerts in the old Queen's Theatre and we attended many of these. You would hear the most famous musicians, world figures like Backhaus, Cortot, Heifetz, Kreisler, Horowitz, Paderewski. Father and mother were fond of the Glasgow Orpheus Choir and never missed one of their concerts. Similarly with John McCormack, who I heard on stage four or five times. There was a great deal more music to be heard in the music halls of Dublin than there is now. But, of course, we now have television.

Our father and indeed his two brothers, Peter (the Carmelite) and Gearóid (the man from Maynooth), all revelled in riddles and tricks, literary ones and others involving cards, matches and coins. Brian was the only one of us to inherit this trait from them and you would suddenly become aware of it at a wedding, at a party or simply when a group were gathered in a pub. At the most inopportune moment when speeches were about to be given, Brian's voice could be heard inviting his immediate companions to observe a trick while coins or matches were presented in some insoluble pattern.

The three of us, the eldest of the family, each received £1 pocket money a month. Today's teenagers would scoff at that, but that £1 was probably worth £5 by today's standards.

There are many kinds of father and they are likely to be as different from one another as people are. There are fathers who explain things and discuss current events with their children almost from the time they attain the use of reason. I hear them at it often enough at the top of the bus! It is probably a good thing in itself and a relatively new phenomenon. It would be foolish to say that our father was like the 'Victorian father', that closed person having no real intercourse with his family you read about in English history and literature. On the other hand, he and we were not garrulous in voicing and discussing our opinions. It was not a question of churlishness – it was our habit or our nature.

I remember how amazed I was the first time I had tea in McManus's house in Stillorgan. Richard McManus was one of Brian's greatest friends but he died young in the early fifties. All through this meal there were arguments going on between the people of the house about current events, while their tea got cold and morsels of food being lifted to their mouths got suspended in mid-air! Some of the participants in these exchanges got excited or angry. I am not suggesting that there was always some kind of row at mealtimes in the McManus household. These occasions were very lively with no stop or ebb in the conversation. That was quite in contrast to the regime in our house – usually we were not particularly talkative or given to voicing opinions. If visitors were in the house our conversation might be more animated, but this would be due to their presence.

Most of the year that I was working on my first novel (*Oíche i nGleann na nGealt*), writing in the same room as my father, it never occurred to me to tell him what I was doing and likewise it didn't occur to him to ask. Today, I suppose, such an occurrence would be labelled 'lack of communication'. By the time the book was published my father was already two years dead. While it is not for me to suggest that he might have approved, it is likely that it would have been of some interest to him since he had an interest in writing himself. It might have pleased him that a son of his who had been raised with Irish had produced some literary work in that language.

He did not live to see Brian's literary flowering. However, an interesting question does arise – did he read any of Brian's work? I'm glad to say that a positive answer can be given to that question.

In 1934 Brian, who was at university at the time, founded a comic periodical called *Blather*. The fun in it was bold and outrageous and contrasts with a more moderate but similar style adopted by him in his later writing. I had little to do with the periodical except that I wrote the odd article for it. It only achieved about six issues; lack of money and the unwillingness of printers to take risks led to its demise.

If we had been asked at the time if our father knew about our having anything to do with this mocking journal, which achieved quite a wide distribution in the shops, we would have answered no – he did not and could not have known. But when we went through his papers after his death, we found he had a copy of every issue.

# 11

IN SPITE OF ALL THE DRIVING that our father did while we lived in Tullamore he cannot have enjoyed it. When we moved to Herbert Place he garaged the Overland in the stables at the back of the house and seldom took it out again. And this was at a time when it was possible to enjoy a trip to the mountains or out of the city in any direction, so free of traffic were the highways and byways. With the Overland gathering dust over a period of nine or twelve months, a local man made some small offer for the car and bought it.

Father used to take us on long walks on Sundays. Leaving Herbert Place we would go in a big arc round to Milltown, from there to Dundrum, thence to the top of Foster's Avenue and down to the Bray Road and in on that road to Donnybrook and home. I remember walking along the Bray road itself rather than on the footpath.

Father did not smoke or drink. Perhaps he would enjoy a few glasses of cider at Christmas time or on some special occasion and accept a cigarette from our uncle Gearóid.

It was difficult to make him angry but the odd thing would provoke him. I remember a telephone call that came late one night, when he was a Commissioner. It was shortly before the budget. I was in bed, but I could hear the conversation quite clearly. I can only guess what was being said at the other end of the line, but it was clear from the sudden change in my father's tone that some attempt was being made to glean information about the new taxes that were to be imposed. The impression I sensed was of astonishment, then outrage and finally white anger – father's voice stammered momentarily with rage and then he took control. It was apparent that the person at the other end of the line was desperately trying to withdraw and excuse himself, but he got no sympathy.

Father was a regular communicant on Sundays and his life at home was quiet and untroubled. However, there must have been considerable tension and worry in the life of a person who raised a big family during that unsettled period in Irish history. If indeed he felt those tensions he showed no trace of it. His life reflected his two baptismal names: Michael and Victor. Michael was reflected in his strength, and Victor in his achievements.

On an evening in July 1937, he, Róisín, Fergus and I were in the sitting-room in the house in Blackrock. The younger sisters, Nuala and Sheila, were also there, and some sort of game developed where our father was laughing and chasing Sheila around the table. He then sat down and resumed reading a book he had put down. In the meantime I had gone up to my own room when I heard Róisín calling urgently to my mother to come at once, that something was seriously amiss. I ran down to investigate. His arm was limp at the side of the armchair, the book fallen from his hand. It was a massive thrombosis. He was dead before a priest or doctor reached him.

He is buried in Deansgrange Cemetery, and my mother and Brian share the same grave.

# 12

IN THE AUTUMN OF 1923, six months after leaving Tullamore and settling in Dublin, Gearóid, Brian and I were sent to school for the first time. Gearóid was fifteen years of age, I was thirteen and a half and Brian was twelve. The Christian Brothers School, Synge Street, was the one chosen for us. Our father did not consult us about going to school or enquire if it was in any way against our principles – he simply announced that the decision had been made. The three of us were put in the same class – Fourth Year – a class that was supervised by Brother Broic. We spent four years in Synge Street, until the family moved house again, this time to Blackrock. Brian remained in Fourth Year for the duration of our time in Synge Street. He sat the Intermediate Certificate, getting honours in that examination. In our last year in Synge Street (1926–7) Gearóid and I were moved up to Fifth Year.

It is very difficult to give an accurate account of the pain we suffered from the huge upheaval in our lives. After the years of complete freedom – with little association with other boys, with no precedent for a stranger having the right to threaten us or give us homework to do, with no habit of preparing lessons or a need to get them right – there are no words to describe the hardship we suffered. One can only compare it to some sort of violence, like throwing a person into the fire or plunging him into freezing water. Indeed, the change affected us so much and we took so long to adjust to our new environment that I would be inclined to say that the price of our earlier freedom had been too high. But on reflection this would be wrong – the halcyon years of freedom were priceless!

The first thing we had to face was the torment that was in store for us from our classmates. They recognized immediately that we were 'green, soft and vulnerable' and decided, as boys will, to have fun at our expense. We were safe as long as we were in the classroom, but in the school yard or at lunchtime things were very different. The whole school, or so it seemed, gathered around us. A lad would approach from behind and give you a push in the back. When you turned to confront him, the boy who was now at your back struck you. It was probably boys from our own class who started this taunting, but boys from other classes soon joined in. They were coming at us from every side and running away again. We could not eat our lunch or do much except put our backs to the wall. Even the walls proved a poor defence as they were low enough for a boy to climb the other side and pull your hair or strike a blow to the head. Of course, the blows were light, but they were none the better for that.

Having suffered this 'persecution' for a number of days I decided to put an end to it. On the following day I went out into the school yard and waited until I saw, out of the corner of my eye, the first boy making for me from behind. As it happened, he was a boy from my own class. Just when he was about to strike me, I rounded on him and struck him a blow to the face with my fist. It was no playful blow and before he had time to recover a crowd had gathered around us. Some older boys intervened and said we could not fight in the yard as the Brothers would intervene. Instead, we were advised to go up a lane on the way home from school to settle matters between us. It was apparent that these boys liked arranging fights and had taken the matter in hand.

When the last class was over, four or five of the older boys accompanied us to the lane, which was off Harrington Street. We abandoned our school bags, threw off our jackets and began fighting. The first blows we exchanged were not very effective and did little damage. Then I succeeded in striking my opponent a hard blow to the nose. As I had no experience in boxing, this blow was a lucky strike. His nose began to bleed so heavily and he was so blinded by a mixture of blood and tears that the fight was over.

From that day on nobody interfered with me. Apart from these early school hazards there were two strong senior boys who posed as the 'Kings' of the school and expected other pupils to obey them – there are bullies like that in every school. The three of us had some trouble with the 'Kings' for a while but eventually we were accepted like any other pupils. An interesting aspect of our assimilation into the world of school is that Brian had no need to employ his fists. He had a characteristic gift that enabled him to come out of such encounters without violence. I noticed this ability of his again, in later life.

One would imagine that we would be far behind in class

*The Bowling Green in Strabane, Co. Tyrone, birthplace of Brian O'Nolan.*

*Main Street, Strabane, in the early years of the century.*

*The terrace of St Michael's, Inchicore, where the O'Nolans lived c. 1914–17.*

*'The Copper Beeches', Tullamore, where the O'Nolans lived 1920–3.*

*In the Blackrock Chess Club: Michael O'Nolan (far right) is playing with A.A. MacDonagh, founder and headmaster of Avoca School.*

*A Union Jack being burned in the garden of the O'Nolan house in Avoca Terrace. From left: Desmond Kenny, Joseph Kenny, Gearóid O'Nolan and Richard McManus. Brian 'was no passive observer in these activities'.*

*Top: The O'Nolan home at 25 Herbert Place, Dublin.*

*Left: The O'Nolan home at 4 Avoca Terrace, Blackrock.*

due to our beginning school so late, but strangely enough we were not. We did not have any Latin but once we started to learn it we were soon as good as anyone else. We had not been introduced to algebra or Euclid before going to Synge Street, but while the rest of the class were no beginners, they were not so advanced that we were not able to catch up quite quickly. We were not great at arithmetic, but were as good as some in the class. When it came to Irish and English we were ahead of the best in the class – we had read far more English literature and our literary appreciation was more mature.

I remember well how distressed I was when required to memorize verses from Macaulay's *The Lays of Ancient Rome*, 'The Stand of Horatio on the Bridge'. I thought, and still do, that it is bad verse. Likewise, I did not agree with having to memorize a poem such as 'The Seagull' by Gerald Griffin. I do not know if Brian was of a like mind on such matters but I guess he would have been – we seldom discussed such things. However, one piece of the English reader which we did discuss, and were of one mind about, was an extract on Marie Antoinette by Edmund Burke. We had much fun with this piece, especially the opening lines, '... and surely never lighted on this orb, which she hardly seemed to touch, a more delightful vision. I saw her just above the horizon ...'. It seemed to us that it was a barrage balloon that was being described! I think Brian satirized this passage in his column in *The Irish Times* long afterwards. It would be unfair, though, to conclude that we were only introduced to third-rate poems and bad prose in Synge Street.

# 13

DURING THE FOUR YEARS we lived in Herbert Place the three of us slept in a room on the fourth floor. It was a big room, the width of the house with two windows. It was the custom at that time to send children to bed early – too early. We used to go upstairs at the appointed time but not to bed. Most nights we played some game or other or occasionally had a good pillow fight. Other nights were spent looking out the window.

One night I let a little piece of paper fall out of my hand and we watched it floating and fluttering down the street. Little things like that make a pastime for the idle. We got more pieces of paper and threw them out the window, and that begot another idea. The following night it was not paper we had up the stairs but stones! They were little stones no bigger than fine gravel. We threw them out and listened to hear how long it took for them to strike the path below. The second night the stones were bigger and we had a plan. We waited until after dark, with the street lamps lit. We kept watch until a pedestrian appeared on the path on the house side of the street. As soon as he had passed the gate, so that there was no danger of him being hit, we threw the stone so as to fall on the path behind him. Imagine the sudden fright a person would get from such a missile, coming as it did from the fourth storey! When the startled pedestrian looked about him there would be nobody to be seen, as Herbert Place was always a quiet street, particularly at night. A clump of trees on the canal bank would seem to be the most likely hiding-place for the blackguard who had thrown the stone.

Comparing the responses to the sudden thud of our missiles provided the excitement and fun for us. Most of the 'victims' stood for a moment before walking off again. There were others who made no delay but hastened their step. Then there would be the odd courageous person who would come back, strike a match and begin searching for the object that had been thrown. That used to tempt us very strongly to throw another stone but we did not yield to temptation – it was too dangerous.

The stone-throwing lasted for perhaps a week. It was destined to come to a sudden end. On the last night I'm not sure how many stones we had already thrown, but the last one was intended for a man coming from the Mount Street direction. When he had gone past we threw the biggest stone in this nocturnal escapade. Whichever of us threw it had to go right back to the far wall and take a run up to the window to get sufficient 'follow-through'. Instead of falling on the path, the stone struck the iron railings that fenced the little lawn at the front of the house. You could hear the 'cling' it made three hundred yards away!

The man stopped on the spot. Instead of looking about him as most of the people did, this man stared straight up at the window where we were hidden in the darkness. He must have been convinced from the sound created by the impact of the stone on the railings that the stone had a vertical rather than horizontal trajectory. He stood for a long time looking up but we were hidden by the black void where the window was open. We watched and waited, thinking he would never move. He did, at last, but instead of passing on up the street, what should he do but turn into the gate of the house next door! He was our neighbour, a dentist named Morewood.

We recognized that we might have made a serious blunder but it did not stop us having the stones ready for action the following night. However, our initial survey of the 'arena' showed that some significant change had taken place. We saw tiny points of light shining under the trees on the far side of the road along the canal bank. This was something new. We spent a long time watching these reflections, which seemed to move from time to time. Then it dawned on us what they were – the reflections from the bright buttons of a policeman's uniform. It was evident that a complaint had been lodged with the law. We did not throw any stones that night or any other night afterwards.

I need hardly tell the reader about my anger now when I read in the newspapers about boys throwing stones – the blackguards – they should be horsewhipped and put in prison! How quickly one forgets one's own youthful indiscretions!

# 14

IN THE AUTUMN OF 1927 we went to live in Blackrock. The house, at Avoca Terrace, is about a mile from the village. Brian, Gearóid and I attended Blackrock College as day students. This was a great change from Synge Street – there was not nearly as much homework to be done, the discipline was easier and the atmosphere more liberal. The Brothers in Synge Street had crammed so much knowledge into our heads that there was no need, for me at any rate, to do any study while I was at Blackrock. Nor did I have to do much study in my first year at university.

In those days Dr John Charles McQuaid, who later became Archbishop of Dublin, was Dean of Studies in Blackrock. He also taught English to the sixth-year A class.

I have often read journalists describing the Archbishop as 'a shy, retiring man' who would be ill at ease in company. This portrayal of the man is totally inaccurate, as he had a strong personality and many boys in the college used to imitate him, not in a mocking fashion, but for the sake of good mimicry. He had an unusual walk, holding one shoulder a little higher than the other. He was soft-spoken and made certain gestures with his hand – all characteristics which the boys noted and imitated. His writing style was very fine, with the letters separated from one another as if printed, and many of the boys, including Brian, copied it. I remember blank spaces in Brian's textbooks carrying imitations of this writing with ideas and expressions that were never likely to occur to Father McQuaid!

Father McQuaid was a good teacher of English. He shared with us his opinion that Hillare Belloc was the best English writer of our time. He used to discuss literary matters with me from time to time and lend me books. I think he may have thought that I had the makings of a good writer in English. As far as I know Brian was never in Father McQuaid's class.

Father McQuaid was later appointed President of the College. 'Mixer' was the nickname the boys had for him: the name came from the pipe tobacco called 'Mick McQuaid'. As I knew him he was a friendly, sociable, learned man with a good sense of humour.

We made new friends both in the College and in Blackrock itself: Richard McManus from Stillorgan, Oscar Quigley who lived opposite the College in Williamstown but did not attend school there, and a family of five boys called Kenny who lived nearby in Avoca Avenue.

We were 'patriotic' in those years and were members of a branch of An Fáinne in Dún Laoghaire. This organization ran monthly *céilithe* and raised money for the Gaelic League by organizing door-to-door collections, and we took part in these activities. Some of our friends, like Richard McManus, were great enthusiasts about the Irish language; others, like Quigley or the Kennys, had no Irish at all.

Dún Laoghaire and its environs was populated at that time by a very pro-British contingent. Some of these people would be provocative and ask the conductor on the tram for a ticket to 'Kingstown', and often you would hear the angry or disrespectful reply. In Dún Laoghaire's main picture house, The Pavilion, when an English newsreel was being shown which featured the Royal Family, there would be derisive clapping.

It was customary for the Union Jack to be flown alongside the flags of other nations whenever there was an event in Dún Laoghaire. We took exception to this practice and took down as many Union Jacks as we could. The Royal George Yacht Club had a large Union Jack flying from the flagstaff of the club, and on one occasion we managed to take this down and burnt it. Brian was no passive observer in these activities.

He also pursued his own personal campaign. It was a rule in Blackrock College that every pupil had to have a college blazer for formal occasions. He discovered that the blazers being sold to the pupils were made in Leeds. He spoke very strongly on the subject at an Irish debate which was chaired by Father O'Mahony, the Professor of Irish.

Dissatisfied with airing the matter orally, he went into the College in dead of night, accompanied by Oscar Quigley, and painted the slogan 'DON'T BUY BRITISH BLAZERS' in two-foot-high letters on the gable end of the handball alley in the quadrangle. Such a protest would cause little impact today but at the time it was a matter of great scandal. The College authorities moved very quickly to remove or blot out the offensive message – the first prose sentence that Brian ever published.

# 15

IT WAS WHILE WE WERE STILL AT SCHOOL in Dublin
that Brian, Gearóid and I first visited the Donegal Gaeltacht.
The year was 1927. We witnessed the end of an era – the way
of life that Séamus Ó Grianna depicts so well in his stories.
Shawls were still being worn by the old women and a good few
of the younger ones too.

It is difficult to describe for a younger generation, who
motor through the wilds of Donegal on fine roads, how different it was then. We usually travelled to Donegal from
Strabane by car. In one place, near Dunfanaghy, the tide used
to come in over the public road. I remember a spot where
there were two big sand banks on the road to the sea – they
were landmarks that could be seen from afar, shining a silvery
white. There is no sign of them today; grasses have grown on
them over the years and hidden the fine white sand.

We rented a house on Cnoc na Bealtaine, about three miles
from Gort an Choirce. The house was probably bigger than
the houses in 'Máire's' stories but similar in many ways.

There was an old woman, a caretaker, in the house – just like the ones you read about in legendary stories like *Peig*. One day when she and I were alone in the kitchen she produced something from her pocket and pressed it into my hand without saying a word. This appears to have been some sort of gesture of kindness that required no communication between giver and recipient. As soon as I could I went to the door to see what I had been given. It was a small piece of meat. I am unable to explain the significance of this – perhaps it had some link with the Famine?

Another experience we had on our first visit to the Gaeltacht was to attend a wake. Clay pipes filled with tobacco were passed around, as was a plate of snuff. At the time I did not know what snuff was so when the plate reached me I made a sign with my hand, imitating what I thought other people were doing.

Another year, 1928 or 1929, Brian and I took our bicycles with us to the Gaeltacht. We cycled to Machaire Rabharta, a place where boat races were held. Here we saw two old men wearing suits made of *glaisín*. They were full suits – trousers, jacket and, if memory serves me right, a hat of the same material. That was the only time we saw the like of that in Donegal.

Attendance at Coláiste Uladh in those days was for adults only, most of them student teachers and university students. And when you combined the visitors with the local people you had a great base for Irish dances. On such gala evenings there would always be a big crowd of local boys clustered outside the door looking into the dance hall. In time the crowd would swell and some would venture inside the hall forming a crescent immediately inside the door, each of them wearing the local costume — a cap! Sooner or later, usually in the lull between dances, someone would snatch the cap from one of these boys and throw it into the middle of the dance floor. It would lie there, with everyone staring at it and the owner too shy to retrieve it.

The local girls spoke Ulster Irish, the language we used at home, so it was with these girls that we associated.

Today you could drive through Gort an Choirce, and I have done so, without finding anything to distinguish it from other towns. It has changed beyond recognition, and I'm not simply thinking of McFadden's Hotel, the church or the college. If the crossroads were not there, maybe I would fail to recognize Falcarra. There was a well, halfway down the hill, where people from that side of the town drew their water. The first time we passed up the hill in 1927 there was a young red-headed girl drawing water; her name was McCarthy and we exchanged greetings. There are rows of houses down to the end of the hill now and the well has been capped. The odd time I go there on short visits I am aware of the physical changes that have occurred, but I grieve more for the language which has declined and for the young generation who were so numerous long ago and are now gone.

# 16

ALTHOUGH IT WAS NOT DARK when we reached Cnoc na Bealtaine in 1927, we did not have enough time to explore our surroundings the first day. The following morning we set out to survey the area. It is a countryside of glens and hills with the bulk of Cnoc Fola forming a backdrop to the sky. The voices of people and the lowing of cattle could be heard from a village far away on the other side of the valley. Nearby one was aware of the murmur of streams and all around us the countryside was bathed in golden yellow sunlight.

A boreen led us to the brow of a hill where our attention was drawn to something out in the middle of a bog. The focus of our attention was an old yellow stone outhouse. This structure was dilapidated and hardly fit for animals. We would not have given this derelict structure a second thought except that smoke was rising from a hole in the thatched roof, proclaiming that somebody lived there. We drew closer to investigate, walking around until we reached the open door. It was so dark inside that nothing could be seen, but we were visible from the inside or our presence had been otherwise sensed. From a bed in a corner of the dark room, a woman's voice began singing a five-worded nonsense rhyme over and over again. I do not know if the song was to challenge us, to let us know that the house was occupied, or simply for fun. Shyness on our part stopped any further exploration so we made a quick getaway.

The following day we saw this woman and I shall never forget the shock we got. The face was old and haggard, like the face of a hag, but it transpired that it may not have been age but the hardship she bore that aged her prematurely. She was of medium height and dressed in the local fashion – a black shawl. What was unusual was that she had only one leg and this was bare. She was going down the road on the one leg in jumps, with no crutch or support of any kind! Even kangaroos have two legs. When she had travelled about thirty yards she took a big jump to one side into the ditch, where she lay resting and getting her breath back. Once she was rested, she got up on the one leg and resumed her journey.

The incident of the 'hopping' woman might have been forgotten had there not been more to it. This poor woman went to mass on Sundays, and from the hovel on the bog to the church in Gort an Choirce is a distance of two miles with steep hills en route. Cnoc na Bealtaine alone is a severe slope. The road also needs to be added to the equation. At the time there were no tarred or tarmacadamed roads in Donegal. The roads, such as they were, contained massive potholes and were covered in sharp stones; in summer they were dusty, in winter they were muddy. A family that lived on the road to Gort an Choirce told me that they regularly saw this woman making her way past, even in winter when there was snow on the ground! Someone else told me that resting in the ditch was not her only stratagem – she would also rest against a tree or a wall!

Gallagher was her name and it is hard to understand how she survived in that hut on the windswept bog. I thought that she lived alone but I have since learned that she had a brother who had the old-age pension, which was worth about five shillings a week.

I met people afterwards who could not understand why she did not use a crutch. If they had seen the 'house' and if they thought of the life that prevailed there, they would quickly appreciate her plight – there were no social services in those days nor any thought of them.

I never found out how she lost the leg or how long she had to live with the affliction. She is dead a long time and buried in the graveyard in Gort an Choirce. I like to think that her brave heart must have given up the struggle in the middle of one of her jumps. If that be so, then who is to say that this last jump didn't take her over the hills into eternity!

# 17

IN 1929 FOUR OF US, Brian, Richard McManus, Thomas Kenny and I, went camping in County Wicklow. We travelled by bicycle and spent a fortnight in Glenmalure, penetrating deep into the glen. Swimming, climbing the mountains and exploring the neighbourhood occupied much of our time and the venture proved to be a good practice run for a far more ambitious camping trip which we planned to undertake the following summer.

The Gaeltacht of Donegal was our target – the intention being to spend a fortnight under canvas there. Five undertook this expedition: Brian, myself, Joseph Kenny and his brother Desmond, who lived near us in Blackrock, and Thomas Kenny, who had been with us in Wicklow but was unrelated to the other Kennys. When we were ready to leave there was so much baggage and equipment loaded on the bicycles that it was difficult to mount them. Joseph and Desmond Kenny enjoyed fowling so they brought two guns with them – a good two-barrelled fowling gun and a .22 rifle. The licences they had for the guns were from the Free State so we were unable to take them across the border. That meant that we could not take the direct route through Monaghan, Strabane and Letterkenny, but would have to cross the country on the south side of the border, approaching Donegal through Bundoran. The planned route would then take us through the Glens, Cloch Liath and Gaoth Dobhair to Gort an Choirce. Our journey's end was to be Gort an Choirce in Cloch Cheannaola – that was the part of the Gaeltacht that we knew best. It was the first visit to the Gaeltacht for the other three and we did not mind the longer journey as we wanted to see that part of the countryside.

The expedition took place in August 1930. We had little money so it had to be carefully managed. None of us were drinking at the time – if we had been it is unlikely that we would have got much farther than Lucan! But we were all smoking and the cigarette that puts the finishing touch to a meal, even if it's only a Woodbine, was almost as important as the meal itself. Many of our meals were simply large quantities of bread and butter washed down with a big can of strong black tea.

I do not remember where we slept the first night; it had been showery during the day so we had not managed to travel very far. We went through Virginia on the second day, having spent some time on the lakeshore en route. By the time we reached Belturbet it was raining again with no sign of a clearance. Somebody told us there was an empty house on the outskirts of the town, so we broke into it and spent the night there. It was a fine big house in good condition and it even had a billiard room.

From Belturbet to Drumshanbo in County Leitrim was a pleasant journey over twisty, hillocky roads, and although it was only a short distance travelled we decided to spent the night there. We asked a policeman if the owner would mind if we camped in the corner of a large field on the bank of the river Shannon. He was a talkative, exuberant man, the sort of man who if asked would it be any harm to set fire to the church would have answered, 'Why in the name of God wouldn't you set it alight?' It was an answer like that we got about the field. 'Why wouldn't you camp there? – What's stopping you?'

However, no sooner was the tent erected in the field when we heard shouts and were confronted by a crowd coming across the field towards us, some of them armed with sticks. As they looked aggressive and were bearing down on us, we moved to meet them, thinking to stall a raid on our camp and our gear. The incident was quickly resolved when they realized we were passing campers. Apparently a week previously half a dozen evangelical preachers had visited the town. They can hardly have been Jehovah's Witnesses – that group had not appeared in Ireland then – but another group of that kind. They had been driven out of town. We never heard whether it was by stick, stone or simply threatening language, but they were told not to return. They had come, like ourselves, on bicycles with lots of baggage, and when we were spotted setting up camp in the field it was assumed that the preachers had returned – what appalling cheek!

Once it was clear that we had nothing to do with the evangelical group, our would-be assailants departed apologetically.

The weather showed no sign of improving. Camping in the floods of rain in a little 'bivy' tent that had barely enough room to allow the five of us to stretch out was far from comfortable. So when we reached Cloneen and heard about another empty house we decided to break in. It was in the middle of the town and surrounded by big trees. On entry it was clear that the house had been unoccupied for many years. The dust, like a layer of fur covering everything, was a quarter of an inch thick in places. We chose one of the rooms upstairs as our base, but the place was so bleak and cold that we thought of setting up the tent in the middle of the floor even though the roof was quite sound. I'm not sure if we used the tent or not but we spent most of our time in this room.

The window of 'our' room was half open, with the result that at twilight the room was invaded by scores of bats. We killed some of them and it was the first time I had an opportunity of examining a bat at close quarters. It had the mouse-like head and fur that I had read about and seen in illustrations. What was extraordinary was the lightness and delicacy of the tiny creature – it was almost like a large butterfly. And a flick of the hand was sufficient to stretch it dead on the floor. The bats did not return the second night – no doubt news spread in their colony that some fierce enemy had taken possession of 'their' room!

This house proved to be unlucky for Brian. One morning when he was shaving, his razor became contaminated with the 'fur' on the shelf in the bathroom – he nicked himself with this dusty razor and an ugly scab developed on his upper lip. Afterwards he spent a year attending a skin specialist in Dublin, trying one ointment after another to try to heal the skin. What vexed Brian most was that he could not come with us to Donegal the following year because he was detained in Dublin attending the doctor.

We spent a total of three days in this house and to pass the time we began to do something that campers rarely bother about – cooking! On the second day, while shopping in the town, I discovered that the owner of the house lived nearby. It is curious that he did not notice the light at night as we had 'our' room well lit with candles. Perhaps he did notice but was reluctant to investigate.

Our departure from Cloneen took us on a back road to Rossinver and Loch Meilbhe. The Kennys wanted to visit this lake, reputed to be the best in Ireland for fishing. They had brought fishing rods and also hoped to bag a few duck. I cannot recall whether they had any success with either the fish or the fowl.

It is difficult now, through the mists of forty years, to remember the people we met on our travels, but one old man impressed us because he had the same outlook as the policeman we had met earlier. If you said you intended to do something he'd say, 'And why wouldn't you?' It seems, on reflection, that it may well have been a shrewd strategy to avoid giving information to strangers.

Another man that we got to know quite well was a small farmer in the neighbourhood of Loch Meilbhe. He lived in a cosy house on a side road near the lake. As it was pouring rain again he allowed us to occupy one of his stables. We spent a couple of nights in his warm kitchen discussing world affairs. He was very proud of his wife's cooking and gave us a pot of her home-made jam. He held Dáil deputies in high esteem – unusual at that time – even in remote rural areas, and said his wife would be able to cook for the best of them!

After a few days in the neighbourhood of Loch Meilbhe the weather brightened and we were able to make the last leg of our journey to Gort an Choirce in a single day. Approaching Gaeltacht territory I always find myself looking around to see if we have reached that border where supposedly everything is a little different – the women more beautiful, the men more manly, the apples redder, the fields greener. However, the line is invisible and the only way you can be sure that you have arrived in the Gaeltacht is to hail somebody on the road and hear their greeting.

It was late at night when we reached Gort an Choirce. We went straight up Cnoc na Bealtaine to Gallagher's house. A field behind the house was chosen to pitch our tent, which necessitated hammering wooden stakes into the ground with a mallet. God knows what the Gallaghers made of these strange noises in the middle of the night!

# 18

ONE OF OUR ADVENTURES IN Cloch Cheannaola that year was to go deer hunting. There were deer in Gleann Bheatha at the time and I believe they are still there. In fact, the deer were so numerous that some of them broke through gaps in the wire fencing around the estate and were a danger to motorists on the road at night.

When the Kennys heard that there were deer in the mountains they were keen to go hunting them. Of course it was necessary to recruit guides who knew the mountain terrain, and also the deer and their haunts. It was important, too, to avoid being caught like the man who foolishly drove his car into the estate a week earlier. One of the keepers noticed the car and contacted the Garda barracks. The poacher was caught on his way home with a deer in the boot of his car! We intended to make our way across the mountain on foot.

We found two men who were willing to act as guides. One was fifty years of age, the other a young man of about our own age. Initially it proved difficult to persuade the older man to undertake the task – he wanted to be certain that we had the capacity and endurance for the walk. 'I would not go across the road with the like of those,' he would say, referring to some other people who had sought him as a guide in the mountains. This middle-aged man was as tough and agile as a goat on the mountain and had the vigour of a motor. He was of rural stock that was once as plentiful as bog cotton – strong, active people who would walk twenty miles as readily as others would walk a couple of hundred yards, or think nothing of journeying fifty miles on foot if the need arose.

Seán MacMeanmain, the author, was one of these long-distance walkers. While I never met him – we exchanged a few letters – I was told by my mother's friend Mary Gallagher that he used regularly walk to Strabane from Castlefin, a journey of thirty miles. It was in her house that he used to stay when visiting Strabane and indeed it was there he was arrested by British police or soldiers, as he recorded in one of his essays. His arrest had nothing to do with whatever nationalist protests were taking place at the time, but arose from his association with Mary Gallagher, who was involved in Cumann na mBan.

Our father, too, had this physical capacity for walking long distances. Some time ago I paid a visit to relations still living in Eiscir Dufaigh in County Tyrone. They told me of a day in 1903 when our father walked from Strabane to see his mother. She was out for the day, so he returned to Strabane the same evening. The double journey would be about thirty miles. Thank God I inherited some of this capacity myself – I needed it, too!

Our deer hunt began at daybreak. There were six in the party – Brian, the two Kennys, the two local men and myself. It is surprising the things we do when young. It never occurred to us to conserve our energy for the long walk by going to bed early. Indeed, we did not go to bed at all – there was a big *céile* in Coláiste Uladh and we spent the night there. And while we ate a hearty breakfast before setting out, there was nothing left to make up a lunch pack.

We met the local men as arranged and set off past the station of Caiseal na gCorr heading for the foot of Errigal. It was along this side of the mountain that we went, on a path high above the shore of Lake Altáin. We reached the wire fence of the Gleann Bheatha estate at last and passed through it.

The wilderness of heather and rocky mountain in Gleann Bheatha is bewildering. I have never revisited the place since and do not know if some path has been made in recent times. The opinion I formed on that day was that the uninitiated could easily go astray and be wandering about, lost for days on end. And if bad weather intervened ...

We walked for a good while before we saw a deer – he was far away and disappeared in the twinkling of an eye. We took a rest break at the lake side – this one was called Loch na mBeadaí, according to our guides. We resumed and walked until midday, when the local men sat down to have their lunch. They offered to share what they had with us but we declined their generous offer. Afterwards we headed up a high mountain and on reaching the summit we could see, far below on the floor of the glen, that noble sight, the big-antlered stag with a dozen doe stepping out behind him. They were so far away that they were in no danger from any shot we might fire.

It was well into the afternoon when we reached an area where the terrain consisted of hillocks and little glens. As we came to the mouth of one of these scattered glens – it was no more than a hundred and fifty yards long – behold, standing at the other end was a young deer! Whoever fired the shot from the .22 rifle scored a direct hit, and the deer fell.

The beauty of the slain animal, with its shapely head, its slender snout and its thick red-brown fur, momentarily rebuked us for taking its life. Until that moment it had not occurred to me how even six of us could carry such a weight of meat for a hundred yards, never mind the fifteen miles we were from home! That problem was quickly resolved – the young man was on his knees, a large knife in his hand. He made a long cut in the animal's stomach and removed the entrails. He then began to cut the deer into quarters and these were placed in sacks that our guides had brought with them. It was evident from the quick, deft way he worked that our young guide was no stranger to butchering deer.

Soon we were facing home with our booty stashed in sacks on our backs. Despite the fact that four of us had been fasting since daybreak, I do not remember any ravenous hunger. Neither did I feel any great tiredness until we reached the top of Lake Altáin again. When I saw the long shoreline of the lake which we had to circle, and thought of the journey that remained beyond the lake, the fatigue hit home suddenly and hard. Once we had the lake behind us, one of our guides said that there was a house on the homeward path and that he knew the people who lived there and perhaps we might get a bite to eat. At first I thought he was joking – we were still deep in mountain terrain with no house to be seen anywhere. However, he was right – after a little while, a house appeared on our right.

We knocked up the inhabitants and got a great welcome once their dog had been silenced. I do not remember, at this lapse of time, how many were in the house besides the father and mother but there were at least two. A big plate of porridge was set in front of each of us, with plenty of milk and butter-milk. In due course we were asked if we would like some more and I am ashamed to say that we said we would!

I have often wondered about this strange event in later years. Imagine this family living in mountain terrain, ten miles from a shop … the family passing the evening until supper time … a large pot of the choicest porridge simmering at the fireside. And then the sudden invasion, as the Danes would have come in a raid on a monastery in the ninth century or like a swarm of locusts descending on people's dwellings in the East – the porridge pot emptied in a couple of minutes and all the milk in the house consumed! Of course, I exaggerate – it was not quite as bad as that.

Porridge at that time was made from meal called 'pin-head' and it was far superior in taste to what passes for porridge today. Nor could this porridge be cooked quickly – it had to be simmered gently for hours. The same lengthy cooking applied to porridge made from yellow meal, and if memory serves me right it was the latter that we got that night in Gleann Bheatha.

It was late at night when we reached home – our tent in Cnoc na Bealtaine. A few days later we gave a piece of the deer to a local woman to cook for us. It is a shame to admit that after all the aches, pain and endurance we had undergone, we could not boast that we had tasted venison! The neighbourly woman had no experience of cooking venison and instead of roasting it, she boiled it! A watery stew containing pieces of scraggy meat was all we got from our deer-hunting adventure. The roast that I sent to my mother suffered a similar fate. While mother was an excellent cook, she had an aversion to game, so she threw our joint of deer into the bin.

Notwithstanding all the hardship, it is necessary for a 'would-be' writer to widen his horizons by adventurous days spent deer-hunting while he is young. That is what William Shakespeare did – isn't it?

# 19

BRIAN WENT TO UNIVERSITY COLLEGE DUBLIN in 1929. Like most students, he took an interest in the Literary and Historical Society, the college's debating society.

Meetings of the society were held at 86 St Stephen's Green, a Georgian building with spacious rooms, high ceilings and wide staircases. There were few politicians, writers or lawyers of that time who did not address a meetings of the L&H or who were not members of the society. Pádraig Pearse, W.B. Yeats, Éamonn de Valera, Seán O'Leary, Tadhg Ó hÉalaithe, Jim Larkin, Isaac Butt and J.P. Mahaffy were some of those who addressed meeting of the L&H. Members of the Society included Thomas MacDonagh, a signatory of the 1916 Proclamation, James Joyce, Art Ó Clérigh and Thomas Kettle.

The meetings were held upstairs in the old Physics Theatre on Saturday nights. It was a small enough room, lit by gas and in need of painting and decorating. On one side there were three or four rows of benches, stepped in tiers with the table for the Auditor and Officers of the Society facing them. The rest of the space was filled with chairs. The theatre accommodated about 200 people but often there would be twice that number present with more standing at the door or on the landing outside (Brian claims there used to be up to 600 standing but I think this figure too high). This group was an important part of the meetings, and it was not because there were no seats inside that they chose to stand at the door. They were there for their own fun and amusement and wanted to be free to leave if the 'crack' was not up to their standard. They made their own judgment on the debate: they would shout from the doorway but they had no proper spokesperson until Brian arrived on the scene.

He gave an account of the crowd at the door in an article published in *Centenary History of the Literary and Historical Society, 1855–1955.*

A seething mass gathered and swayed in a very large lobby outside the theatre, some sat on the stairs smoking, and groups adjourned to other apartments from time to time for a hand of cards. Many students participated in the Society's transactions from the exterior of the lobby by choice, for once inside there was no getting out. A particular reason why many remained outside was the necessity to be free to make periodical trips to the Winter Palace at the corner of Harcourt Street, a pub where it was possible to drink three or four strong pints at seven pence each.

This most heterogeneous congregation, reeling about, shouting and singing in the Hogarthian pallor of a single gas-jet (when somebody had not thought fit to extinguish the same) came to be known as the mob, and I had the honour to be acknowledged its President.

Brian attained the title of 'President' with his voice during his first term at university. At that stage he had not put pen to paper. I was in the 'mob' the first night he began to introduce himself. He interrupted the speakers on their feet inside with a shouted addendum or an opportune reference or a play on words. The audience responded with a laugh every time. I myself tried to interrupt in a similar way but I failed to raise a laugh. The second Saturday he was back again. After a couple of weeks this voice from the mob became a necessary feature of the proceedings. Nobody knew him as yet, he was out of sight in the middle of the crowd, but by degrees the voice was identified with its owner. In the end, although this may not have happened during the first year, he went into the theatre and began to speak himself from the benches. I am not certain if the mob was too pleased with this move and I wondered about it myself. It seemed like a surrender to mediocrity and authority. On the other hand, many considered that the 'mob' had a 'deputy' inside the theatre who would speak on their behalf when there was a need to do so, and one who would not put up with any nonsense.

On the landing where the mob stood there was a 'secret' spiral stairway which twisted its way down to the basement and up to the top of the house, giving access to every floor. This stairway was very useful when a 'reception' was being planned for the chairman of the debate. The chairman was always a person of importance in the world outside. There were very few chairmen who knew anything about the L&H who would not be expecting some carefully contrived 'reception'.

I remember going up the spiral stairs one Saturday night to the big empty room directly above the L&H room. A young man was there, on his knees in the twilight. He had taken up a couple of floorboards and was working by candlelight trying to make a hole that would let a shower of water cascade down on

to the chairman's head! There were many such pranks perpe-
trated on visiting chairmen and none of them took exception
except for one man, a professor from the college, who got very
red in the face with anger and walked out.

One night when the debate was in full swing and Brian
interrupting as usual, there was a small group working hard at
the door, which was folded back. Their objective was to take
the door off its hinges. The door, which consisted of two
hinged leaves, was very high and very heavy. They succeeded in
taking off one leaf and this huge door was passed overhead
from hand to hand as though it was proposed to let it fall into
the theatre. Some sensible person, realizing that the weight
could easily crush somebody if it were dropped in the middle
of the crowd, persuaded them to lower the door and restore
it to its hinges.

Brian progressed as a speaker in the society. I don't
remember being present when he was speaking formally but it
appears that he was a comic speaker. P.J. Donovan had this to
say in the *Centenary History*:

None of us will ever forget the debating genius of Brian O'Nolan who
was the best impromptu speaker the Society knew in those days,
because from the first all his speeches were impromptu and likely to
contain a sharp barb even for an unwary chairman attempting to bring
him to order.

A past Auditor of the Society, R.N. Coake, adds:

O'Nolan was undoubtedly the best humorous speaker of my time. I feel
certain that he never prepared a speech or made the most exiguous
note for a speech in his life, but I have seen him, I think in [Vivion] de
Valera's year, hold the house alternately convulsed with laughter and

almost shamefaced with pathos for a full fifteen minutes. In an impromptu debate he was given the subject, after he had stood up to speak: 'Sweet are the Uses of Advertisement'. He said nothing for half a minute while he felt in the outside pockets of his overcoat and then drew from the breast pocket a crumpled copy of the *Evening Herald*. Unrolling the paper slowly, he looked through it until he came to the advertisement for Lux soap flakes and read the headline aloud – 'I wonder does he see that faded slip'. From then on he dealt with the ludicrous aspects of the advertisement with occasional references to the text while the house shook with laughter, but almost imperceptibly he changed the line and analysed the danger of such advertising with a thoughtful penetration [of which] few would have thought him capable.

Not surprisingly, Brian won the medal for impromptu debate for the year 1931–2. He was selected on the team of speakers who were sent to England to debate against some of the universities over there. In 1932–3 he contested the election for Auditor of the Society with Vivion de Valera, but failed to get sufficient support.

During our early years in college, a room was made available to the OTC – the Army Officers Training Corps of the National Army. This room was downstairs near the Main Hall. On the morning that the room was to be formally opened, Brian and I and a small group of students went down to see what was happening. It's likely that some high-ranking army officers were present to make speeches. In the event, it was not they who made the speeches; before anyone had time to say anything, Frank Ryan arrived down the stairs accompanied by a couple of men. This was the Frank Ryan of the IRA who went to Spain to fight against Franco and died in Dresden in 1944. He was a graduate of the university and so had every right to be present that morning. He swept the enlistment and explanatory leaflets off the table with a stick and began to speak, condemning the foundation of the Corps. That was the first time Brian and I saw him, although we knew quite a lot about him. He was the editor of *An Phoblacht* at the time and it was a paper we read. Few issues of the paper appeared that didn't give an account of Ryan being harassed by detectives from the Castle or of attempts to arrest him. A trick he used to resist arrest was to throw himself on the ground and refuse to get up. One had the impression that there were not many streets in Dublin where he had not prostrated himself at one time or another. With that sort of reputation one might expect to see an unkempt person, dirty from the mud of the streets, but far from it; Ryan wore a good grey suit. His face was full, he had the appearance of someone beginning to fall into flesh. Nevertheless, he was a handsome, well-built man and he spoke well. I do not remember what he said and I'm sure that neither Brian nor the other students paid much attention either. His protest failed to strike a chord of sympathy among the student body.

Poor Frank Ryan! I believe he was a good Gaeilgeoir, a rare thing in the IRA.

Brian and I often spoke with students and graduates who were members of the IRA. You would come across these people in the Main Hall. Mícheál Ó Ceallaigh was one of them – he was a big man who used to speak out of the corner of his mouth. He had a grouse that he was being refused leave to do his MA thesis on John Mitchel's prose. I sympathized with him about his predicament but in my opinion whatever professor considered that John Mitchel's prose was not good enough as a subject for a thesis was probably right. Anyway, if Ó Ceallaigh wanted to be so nationalistic, why not go a step further and do his thesis in Irish?

A group within the university opposed 'Remembrance Day', a memorial to those killed in the First World War. That memorial is practically discontinued now but at the time it was a big affair and West Britons used it to proclaim their anti-Irishness. Quite a few graduates and undergraduates used to come in on the 11th of November wearing poppies. While I objected to the practice, I was not prepared to snatch the poppies off their coats as some of the protesters did. However, my attitude must have been observed and my disposition noted, for one day after a lecture in one of the theatres upstairs I was approached by a tall man. He was a native Irish-speaker from Donegal whom I never suspected of having links with the IRA. 'Did you ever think of enlisting in the IRA?' he asked in a low tone. 'I did NOT,' I answered, with emphasis that left him in no doubt. He did not raise the matter again.

Whatever faults UCD had then, the students who had not much time to waste attending lectures – and there were many in this category – were not denied some recreation. A billiard room was available downstairs near the men's cloakroom. The billiard room contained two full-size tables and two smaller ones. On entering it the newcomer would be confronted by an amazing sight – each of the players wearing a hard black hat well back on his head or pulled down over his eyes if he were stretching across the table, taking a shot. This extraordinary sight had a simple explanation. At the time it was customary for clerical students from Clonliffe to wear hats, indeed it was one of the sights of the city to see a group of them walking along in this get-up. Each had a wooden locker in the cloak-room near the billiard room where they kept their hats and other things under lock and key while attending lectures. An idle student decided one day to see what would happen if a firework called a 'slap-bang' were inserted into the key-hole of a locker and ignited. In the event, the lock broke and the door swung open, revealing the black hat sitting on a pile of books. The 'safe-cracker' took the hat and went off to play a game of snooker. Not surprisingly, his distinctive headwear made other players jealous. At the time a slap-bang cost only a few pence so within a short interval each of the players had procured his own hat. I do not think that the clerical students ever discovered what happened, as they did not frequent the billiard room.

For students who had no inclination to play snooker or no money to buy a few glasses of beer in Grogan's pub on the corner, there was a spacious 'reading room' provided so that they were not reduced to attending lectures to pass the time. This reading room had plenty of tables and chairs. Morning papers and some other publications were supplied. This room was used principally for playing poker – schools of poker went on from morning to night. Students arriving in the morning made straight for this room and sat down at one of the tables. On one occasion, five aces were found in the pack that was in use in a school where bets were going very high. A terrific row ensued, the cards were thrown up in the air and that corner of the room set on fire!

We, too, enjoyed gambling, as most of our age-group did, but we avoided playing in College. The stakes were far too high and if you lost in the earlier hands, a thing that can happen to anyone, you had little or no chance of recovering your losses. In any event, card-playing was not a priority for us. Where to get sufficient tobacco for the day was a major preoccupation for young men with little money. I often lay in bed in the morning, facing a day without cigarettes and wondering if it was worth getting up at all. And indeed if I did not get up, would my mother be foolish enough to bring meals upstairs to a body that was fit and showed no signs of sickness?

Brian caused great jealousy by making an astute move during those penurious student years. Through knowing the right people he was appointed to be on the gate at the Phoenix Park Racecourse every Saturday night. The College students had some admission privilege and he was there to identify them from the general public. He received thirty shillings an hour for just standing there – money for nothing, or so we thought. That 'income' was a large sum in those days.

# 20

DURING OUR COLLEGE DAYS we were likely to be in one of four houses: McManus's in Stillorgan; Kenny's ('Rosemount'), opposite the back gate of Carysfort Training College; the house of the lawyer John P. Dunne, 'Ben Inagh' on the Rock Road; or Quigley's in Williamstown.

'Cúl Garbh' was the name of McManus's house in Stillorgan. Their father had spent a good part of his life in South Africa etching photographic printing blocks, a business which he transferred to Dublin on his return home. There were five sons: Seán, Kevin, Bernard, Richard and Peter. There were three daughters. Richard was the one we were especially close to – he was a well-rounded person, generous, intelligent and very tolerant. His talents extended to being a good counsellor on worldly matters and a good judge of literary work. I remember when 'Crúiskeen Lawn' was about to be launched he and Brian spent a couple of evenings closeted in deep discussion. I never met anyone who had so many friends and acquaintances, or who would stand so long in the street talking to them. You could pass him in the street and come by an hour later and he would be still there talking to the friend he had met. Richard and Brian shared a common characteristic – a tenacity that seemed to prevent either of them conceding anything in an argument. I often heard the two of them pursuing some argument for well over an hour, making fun of one another's points, twisting and turning, changing to new ground when it was no longer possible to defend the old one. Eventually they would drive the rest of us to tell them to shut up or go to hell! I never heard Brian admitting that he was wrong in anything he had said.

Many of these arguments and the sorting out of world affairs took place in Keegan's pub in Williamstown, which we patronized largely because it was a dozen yards from Quigley's house at 1 Seafort Parade. At the time we did not know, and it would have been of interest to us if we had, that it was in Keegan's that Michael Collins used to meet the men from the unit he had in Dún Laoghaire.

Quigley's house proved to be a good centre for recreation. We played poker and chess there on Sunday mornings and it was there that we met Koltanowski and his wife.

East of Quigley's house, the sea is only fifty yards away on the other side of the railway line. At full tide the water is deep enough to dive from a concrete platform that is there, but nobody swims there any more because of the pollution in Dublin Bay. Nearby there is a Martello tower – an ideal venue had we wanted to imitate Joyce, but we never succeeded in getting inside it.

'Hunting' flatfish was another of the activities associated with Quigley's house. To engage in this sport you would equip yourself with a spear. This was done by cutting a piece of the wire which fenced the railway line and sharpening one end while forming a handle with the other. I regret to say that the railway company was never consulted or its permission sought for this larceny. Once equipped with a spear, fishing could begin.

At low tide along the east coast the tide goes out until it is only a blue line on the horizon. Although you would hardly notice them, there are shallow pools and the odd stream between the land and the faraway tide. Barefooted with trousers rolled up, you set off for one of these pools. Once in the pool with the water coming up your calf, you agitate the water with your feet. Suddenly you will see, perhaps only five yards away, a flatfish that had been resting on the sand take fright and scurry away. As soon as this happens, you agitate the sand under your feet to raise a cloud of sand in the water. Once the cloud has been raised, the fleeing fish returns, seeing it as an ideal hiding-place. The fish will come and lie in the sand at your feet where the cloud of sand is at its thickest. Often you will feel the presence of the fish as it tries to burrow under your feet. All you have to do to land your fish is to spear it, taking good care not to impale one of your own feet. Experience has shown that the flatfish always come back and seek refuge in the sand storm.

Early in the 1950s Richard McManus died aged only forty. His loss was sorely felt by Brian – the two were very close friends.

After taking his basic degree with honours, Brian did an MA. He did his thesis in Irish – 'Irish Nature Poetry' was the title. It runs to about 20,000 words not including the anthology. I have examined the thesis and it is clear that his aim was to get his degree so as to enhance his career prospects as he intended to apply for a post in the Civil Service. The Civil Service job materialized in 1935; in the meantime he stayed around the university.

# 21

IN AUGUST 1934, to amuse himself, Brian founded a comic periodical called *Blather*. *Blather* purported to be 'The Only Paper Exclusively Devoted to Clay-Pigeon Shooting in Ireland'. It came out monthly and lasted six months. The office was on the second floor of 68 Dame Street. The paper's own version of its address was 68 Blather Street, Blather Cliath!

The following is an extract from the Editor's introduction in the first issue:

*Blather* is here.

As we advance to make our bow, you will look in vain for signs of servility or for any evidence of a desire to please. We are an arrogant and depraved body of men. We are as proud as bantams and as vain as peacocks.

'*Blather* doesn't care.' A sardonic laugh escapes us as we bow, cruel and cynical hounds that we are. It is a terrible laugh, the laugh of lost men. Do you get the smell of porter?

*Blather* is not to be confused with Ireland's National Newspaper, still less with Ireland's Greatest Newspaper. *Blather* is not an organ of

Independent opinion, nor is Ireland more to us than Republic, Kingdom or Commonwealth. *Blather* is a publication of the Gutter, the King Rat of the Irish Press, the paper that will achieve entirely new levels in everything that is contemptible, despicable and unspeakable in contemporary journalism ...

In regard to politics, all our rat-like cunning will be directed towards making Ireland fit for the depraved readers of *Blather* to live in ...

We have probably said enough, perhaps too much.

Anyhow, you have got a rough idea of the desperate class of men you are up against. Maybe you don't like us?

A lot we care what you think.

The style is poor enough – it was modelled on an English comic paper called *Rossle* which like *Blather* had only a brief life. If one were to judge this as the work of a young man who aspired to serious writing in the future, you might conclude that there would not be much fame in store for him. But a perceptive eye would see the aptitude behind it. The style is completely consistent, and there is a sureness of touch in the handling of the material. It is not allowed to degenerate from its base source – that would present a danger that I came to recognize. I wrote some articles for *Blather*, in English of course, which stayed within the *Blather* format but were woefully clumsy. It gave me considerable amusement later when an American author attributed two of my articles to Brian and took such meanings out of them as indications of the qualities that were to blossom in his books!

Brian was already portraying in *Blather* an aspect of that humour which later evoked many laughs in 'Crúiskeen Lawn', the photographs and diagrams taken from old books to which he would attach a ridiculous meaning. There was a 'competition' in the first issue of *Blather* in which the reader was asked to put the right name to pictures of well-known people.

Éamonn de Valera's name appears under a photograph of a man who is as unlike him as he could possibly be. This man has a tin kettle tied to the top of his head with a cord. Under the correct photo of de Valera is the caption, 'Mr Silas P. Hotchkiss, President of the Clanbrassil Street Brass Fender Founders and Tinsmiths' Protection Association, Inc.' The third picture carried a half-romantic literary reference and proved to be the choicest of the three. It showed a man with a straw hat in a Victorian suit sitting on a very high three-wheeler, the wheels of which were a few inches into the sea. It was captioned: 'A beautiful mezzotint showing O'Blather going to call the cattle home across the sand of Dee.'

One can see some foreshadowing of his work in the *Irish Times* in the first verse of a poem which makes fun of Anglo-Irish words:

> O come out, my shillelagh, come out, love, with me,
> On yon smooth cruiskeen lawn we will dance the banshee,
> Or while the moon, lofty Shannon above,
> Through the groves of Nabocklish we'll lovingly rove …

How many sales the six issues of *Blather* achieved in its short life is a long-lost statistic.

# 22

I OFTEN WONDER what Brian would say if he returned and saw that students in America and Europe were writing theses on his work. In his own time he made fun of all the scrutiny and analysis that surrounded the work of James Joyce. Brian's manuscripts have been bought by the Americans and most of them are in safe keeping in American universities. I myself do not believe that Brian will ever become the subject of as much study as Joyce and Yeats are – he is not sufficiently mellow. There is not sufficient difficulty, obscurity and doubtful references in his writing to provide food for research by swarms of 'literary beetles'! The romantic tales and poetic Gaelic place-names often peep over the hedge in the English of Joyce and Yeats like strange flowers from another garden. Brian's work is quite different – he knew both languages well from child-hood, he wrote in both as suited him but he kept them separated from one another. Like the Gael always, as compared to the Anglo-Gael, his speech is hard and direct without any wisps of Celtic mist floating around his words.

There are other reasons why he should not be treated like a body on an operating table for exploration by the 'literary beetles'. There is no need to explain real humour; to do so is to spoil it. I have seen articles running to a couple of thousand words of tortuous terminology to explain something, when an author's flash of humour has already lit up the sky like a flash of lightning! It occurs to me to question the right of the blind to be tutoring those who can see perfectly. It would matter little, all this heavy study and 'scholarship', were it not for the fact that it frequently misleads ordinary readers.

I have read repeatedly that *An Béal Bocht* is a satire – it is nothing of the kind. Common sense and evidence of the author's enjoyment of his regular visits to the Gaeltacht preclude any suggestion of a parody on the Gaeltacht or its people.

People often ask – if *An Béal Bocht* is not satire, then what is it? I would see it as a piece of natural exuberance – fun for the sake of fun – like the playfulness of a puppy! But people of deep learning are always searching for other meanings behind something that is simple and easy to understand in the first place. It is a pity they do not ask themselves what motivates them to keep seeking 'hidden' meanings; then we might be rid of them for once and for all! A spontaneous laugh, whether caused by simple happiness or the recall of an amusing incident, according to the 'experts' merits immediate and thorough investigation.

*An Béal Bocht* was written by Brian when he was young and had that rapier-like sense of humour which made its first appearance in *Blather*. He had been reading or re-reading *An t-Oileánach* at the time and this was a book which he very much admired, so *An Béal Bocht* has its roots in exuberance, not malice.

107

# 23

'NOBODY ARRIVES INTO THIS WORLD with his craft,' says Seosamh Mac Grianna at the beginning of *Pádraic Ó Conaire and Other Essays*, in which he gives an account of the first essays he wrote himself but did not publish. It is probable that he is right in this assertion, but it seems that not everybody follows the same path in learning how to handle thoughts and then expressing them in words. Perhaps the craft of communications is learned in the memory or from reading – in any event I cannot contradict Niall Sheridan when he comments on Brian's first essays in his university days: 'Looking back, it seems to me that he burst onto the scene fully equipped as a writer' (*Myles: Portrait of Brian O'Nolan*). If Brian had been engaged in writing unpublished work before going to university, it is hard to see how I would not have been aware of it – it was usual for us to go around together and to discuss whatever we were doing. Further, we slept in the same room – the long back room on the third floor of the house in Avoca Terrace. It was in that room that Brian did almost all of his early writing, on a table which he made himself and placed near the small window. The table, I fear, would not get any awards in a carpentry class in a vocational school, but it was strong and functional. That table witnessed the creation of *At Swim-Two-Birds*, *An Béal Bocht* and *The Third Policeman*. He made another table, an even cruder one, to put at his bedside for books.

While on the subject of this back bedroom, I recall that it had a 'púca' or ghost – and I don't mean the 'Púca Mac Feilimí'! Donal Bán O Céilleachair tells about a púca that used to be around his own locality in Cúl Aodha, called 'An Béiceachán', that used to scream like a bullock being confronted by a butcher. Our púca belonged to a like tribe – a crack in the door jamb was responsible for the screaming. On windy nights when a draught went down the stairs it would cause a piece of wallpaper near this crack to vibrate and give tongue to a deep scream that would last for a few seconds and then subside. This *béiceachán* would not always scream when expected – on many a windy night he would remain silent. Then, unexpectedly, on a night when the wind was not so strong he would start screaming again. I used to enjoy listening for the púca, but Brian didn't take any interest in the púca's nocturnal disturbances.

Like almost every writer, Brian began to write with pen and paper. However, for many years subsequently he did his composition directly on the typewriter. It was very seldom that he made a correction or re-wrote a sentence. He was a writer who wrote easily, without any mental difficulty. He never seemed to re-read what he had written other than to glance at the text as he typed it.

It is hard to define a point in time when one's youth is over and adulthood takes over. In writing this memoir I planned to follow Brian through to his days in university and leave it at that. It is not for me to make a judgment on his work or his life. At the time I am recalling, the university period, he talked of owning a provincial newspaper. I do not know what exactly he had in mind but he mentioned it more than once. He mentioned the subject again when he was working in the Civil Service and probably enjoyed a fair amount of free time. Perhaps the smaller provincial paper, free of the problems and costs of a big newspaper, appealed to him as a base on which he could develop a new kind of paper, the like of which had never been seen before – who knows?